W9-ACV-930

PIE FOR EVERYONE

PIE FOR EVERYONE

Recipes and Stories from
PETEE'S PIE,
New York's Best Pie Shop

Petra "Petee" Paredez

Photography by Victor Garzon

ABRAMS, NEW YORK

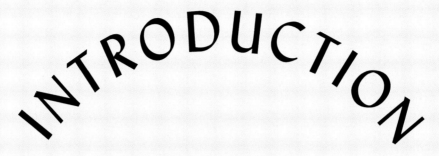

INTRODUCTION

PIE FOUNDATIONS

THE RECIPES

RECIPE LIST

CRUSTS & CRUMBS

BUTTER PASTRY DOUGH 38

VEGAN PASTRY DOUGH 39

CORN PASTRY DOUGH 39

GLUTEN-FREE PASTRY DOUGH 39

RYE PASTRY DOUGH 40

LARD PASTRY DOUGH 40

WHOLE-WHEAT PASTRY DOUGH 40

EGG WASH 56

CORNMEAL-PECAN CRUMB 58

BROWN BUTTER
HAZELNUT-ALMOND STREUSEL 59

CHOCOLATE GANACHE
FOR BLACK-BOTTOM PIES 62

SUGAR SCRAPS 63

BAKED FRUIT PIES

RHUBARB PIE 66

STRAWBERRY-RHUBARB PIE 68

JUNEBERRY PIE 70

SUMMER PEACH (OR NECTARINE) PIE 72

AUTUMN PEACH (OR NECTARINE) PIE 74

SOUR CHERRY PIE 76

BLACK CURRANT PIE 82

WILD BLUEBERRY PIE 88

MAPLE–WILD BLUEBERRY PIE 90

AUTUMN PEAR PIE 92

CLASSIC APPLE PIE 98

MAPLE-BUTTER APPLE PIE 100

STONE FRUIT & BERRY PIES 102

MINCE PIE 105

CHILLED PIES

COCONUT CREAM PIE 110

CHOCOLATE CREAM PIE 113

SPRING CORDIAL PIE 116

COFFEE CREAM PIE 119

BANANA CREAM PIE 122

LEMON MERINGUE PIE 128

KEY LIME MERINGUE PIE 130

NESSELRODE PIES 136

PISTACHIO CLOUD PIE 138

BERRY DREAM PIE 141

CHEESECAKE 146

BUTTERSCOTCH CREAM PIE 149

HONEY CHÈVRE PIE 152

CUSTARD, CHESS & NUT PIES

CUSTARD PIES 158

COCONUT CUSTARD 159

EGG CUSTARD 159

ORANGE CUSTARD 159

CARAMEL CUSTARD 160

CARDAMOM·ROSE CUSTARD 160

PERSIMMON PUDDING PIE 162

SWEET POTATO PIE 164

PUMPKIN PIE 170

CAJETA MARLBOROUGH PIE 172

SALTY CHOCOLATE CHESS PIE 176

LEMON CHESS PIE 178

ALMOND CHESS PIE 180

CHESTNUT RUM CHESS PIE 182

SESAME CHESS PIE 184

MEYER LEMON SUNSHINE PIE 186

CAJETA MACADAMIA PIE 188

BROWN BUTTER–HONEY PECAN PIE 190

MAPLE·WHISKEY WALNUT PIE 192

PONY PIE 194

VEGAN PUMPKIN PIE 196

VEGAN PECAN PIE 197

SAVORY PIES & QUICHES

TOMATO RICOTTA PIE 200

CHEESE & ONION PIE 202

CHILE VERDE PORK PIE 204

SAVORY MINCEMEAT PIE 206

MEAT & POTATO PIE 208

CHESHIRE PORK PIE 210

QUICHE 216

CHICKEN POT PIES 220

À LA MODE

TOPPINGS & OTHER DELICIOUS HOMEMADE PIE INGREDIENTS

BUTTERSCOTCH SAUCE 225

CAJETA 226

CHOCOLATE FUDGE 226

CUSTARD SAUCE 227

MACERATED CHERRIES 228

MAPLE WHIPPED CREAM 228

SOUR CHERRY OR WILD BLUEBERRY SAUCE 229

VANILLA BEAN ICE CREAM 229

EVAPORATED MILK 230

SWEETENED CONDENSED MILK 230

VANILLA SEA SALT MERINGUE 231

VANILLA WHIPPED CREAM 231

INTRODUCTION

WHY WE MAKE PIE

Americans really seem to think that pie is ours.

After all, pie is a staple of the American aesthetic, from Norman Rockwell to David Lynch, and it is the crucial culmination of the most American of holidays, Thanksgiving. However, depending on how generous your definition is, pie has existed for millennia.

Culinary historians posit that ancient Egyptians transported honey, nuts, and fruit in a baked dough and that this tradition was passed on to the Greeks, who baked meats in a simple flour-water pastry. Pie was popular in ancient Rome, too—a dish called *placenta* involved sheep's cheese and honey baked in a wheat and spelt crust. Where Roman roads led, pies spread. Cooks in the various regions of Europe took to the crust-and-filling combination and incorporated it into their culinary repertory.

The early English pies were more functional than decadent. Although the crust—known as a *coffyn*—was made of flour, it was tough to the point of inedibility, meant to be used as a baking vessel and storage container for the cooked filling. The Dark Ages of pie were temporary, though, as the English are also credited for incorporating fat into the crust, inventing a short pastry that was indeed tender enough to enjoy.

The English were responsible for yet another wave of pie proliferation. Pie is now central to the culinary identity of the many nations born of England's imperial pursuits—consider the meat pies of Australia and New Zealand and the phrase "as American as apple pie." Where the English colonists landed, so did pie. From there the regional permutations—sweet, savory, and in between—emerged. This begets the question: Why is it that when I talk about pie, I'm most likely referring to dessert, while in England the mention of pie might signify a savory meal? Like so many peculiarities of American culture,

Pies at a Fourth of July barbecue in Callicoon, New York: Cheesecake, Strawberry Dream, Juneberry, Chocolate Cream, and Key Lime

the answer can be traced to the dark and shameful heart of our capitalist foundation, slavery.

Sugarcane was first cultivated in Asia and first refined in India. The practice spread west into Persia, then both refined sugar and the knowledge of how to make it spread even farther, with the Arab expansion in the seventh century. After it reached the Iberian peninsula, Christopher Columbus brought sugarcane to Hispaniola, the Portuguese brought it to Brazil, and the Dutch dispersed it throughout the West Indies. Slave labor fueled the sugar industry, and sugar processing became more efficient and less wasteful, making crystallized sugar more widely available and cheaper than ever before. In the early eighteenth century, the American colonies functioned as a trading hub between the West Indies and Europe. By the mid-nineteenth century, sugar cultivation spread into North America, until plantations along the Mississippi River were supplying roughly 25 percent of the world's sugar (of course, it was available to the fledgling American states as well). With all that sugar at their disposal, it's not surprising that American tastes in pie turned sweet.

American author and abolitionist Harriet Beecher Stowe once wrote of pies in the era of the sugar boom:

> The making of pies at this period assumed vast proportions that verged upon the sublime. Pies were made by forties and fifties and hundreds, and made of everything on the earth and under the earth.
>
> The pie is an English institution that, when planted on American soil, forthwith ran rampant and burst forth into an untold variety of genera and species. Not merely the old traditional mince pie but a thousand strictly American seedlings from that main stock evinced the power of American housewives to adapt old institutions to new uses. Pumpkin pies, cranberry pies, huckleberry pies, cherry pies, green-currant pies, peach, pear, and plum pies, custard pies, apple pies, Marlborough-pudding pies, pies with top crusts and pies without, pies adorned with all sorts of fanciful flutings and architectural strips laid across and around and otherwise varied all attested the boundless fertility of the feminine mind, when once let loose in a given direction.

Indeed, the pie is a culinary vehicle that can travel across millennia and seasons, that can adapt so adeptly to a region's cuisine that we all want to claim it as our unique tradition and gastronomic rite. Making pie is an inherently generous act, because pie is a dish meant to be shared. It has the power to transform a meal into a celebration and friends into family.

Sadly, despite the unprecedented availability of fine ingredients now at our fingertips, people often encounter pie in such compromised renditions that something that should be objectively good—butter pastry baked with spiced, sweetened fruit, for example—provokes the response, "I'm not really a pie person." We are *all* pie people; we just have yet to find the perfect pie. And to find the perfect pie, you might have to make it yourself—which is something I know a little about.

A late summer visit to Lost Corner Farm, where my family lives and works.

GROWING UP IN A BAKING AND FARMING FAMILY

I grew up in a pie business that my parents started in 1981,

when my oldest sister was a baby. They didn't have secure housing at the time, and the farm they'd been operating along with my uncle went under after a loan they were depending on failed to come through. They had to figure out some way to make ends meet. So they rented a house and started baking pies in the kitchen to sell at a local farmers' market. Their pies were a hit, and the market owner declared that they needed a brand. This was not something my parents had considered. Knowing that people associated pies with both maternal tenderness and patriotic sentiment—and also knowing that there was some irony that they, the pie makers, were destitute hippies who didn't exactly align with that image—they decided to call their enterprise Mom's Apple Pie Company.

By the time I was born, four years after my parents started making pies, their business was not merely a bakery—it was a pie factory. They started to specialize: My dad became the head baker and directed his crew, while my mom handled the business end and sought out new markets. The factory was brimming with endless stacks of hundred-pound sacks of sugar, cornstarch, and flour lining the cinderblock walls. There was a mesmerizing dough mixer that could fit me and all my siblings inside, and a twelve-foot-tall apple peeler that whirred apples around in four little saucers and spiraled their peels to the floor. There were two gigantic ovens with shelves that rotated in a Ferris wheel fashion that my dad sometimes had to climb inside to fix. He'd emerge covered in soot, sweaty, and beet red.

Perhaps the "pie line" was the most interesting of all the machinery. My dad got it secondhand from an old pie factory in Ottumwa, Iowa, and had it trucked down to Virginia. It was covered with so much grease, flour, and rust that he spent $7,000 to sandblast it clean. With

We opened our Lower East Side shop on a shoestring budget in 2014.

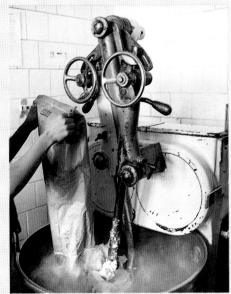

Above: On a warm day we open the window, and the smell of baking butter wafts into the street. Above right: Our mesmerizing Artofex dough mixer, a junior version of the one at my parents' bakery, is a true workhorse.

it, they began mass-producing the most delicious pies possible, in quantities sufficient to populate the bakery aisles of all the grocery stores in the Northern Virginia/DC metropolitan area. It rolled out sheets of my dad's tender dough onto aluminum pie tins, deposited glops of fruit filling from a funnel-shaped vat, layered on a top crust, then punched a crimped design around the crust's edge, which my dad had carved to look like his fat-fingered crimps. Even though he was dead set on making vast numbers of pies as efficiently as possible, he also knew that his personal imprint, chunky and imperfect, conveyed his humble devotion to the art of pie.

We ordered pie any time we saw it on a menu, then dissected it as a family. When it comes to pie and produce, my father has a mad-professor energy about him—a zeal and fervor that makes his pastry appraisals hard to dismiss. So while it might have been odd for an outsider to observe this unusual exercise, I took in his doctrine with rapt pride. He would examine the crust—did it flake, did it crumble, or did it peel back like leather? Was the bottom fully baked or was it pasty and waterlogged? Did they use ripe fruit in the filling, or was it flavorless, further diminished by the heat of the oven? Much of the time he'd take a bite and purse his lips, looking down at the plate with a silence that spoke volumes.

When we had disappointing pie, my dad took that as a sign of the times. When it came to quality and flavor, the eighties and nineties were not exactly the Golden Age of agriculture. My dad grew up in a frugal family of eleven. My grandfather wasn't a farmer, per se—throughout my father's childhood he worked as a quality control expert for the military—but he came from agrarian stock and his family had a very large, functional garden that supplied most of their meals. Thus, my dad knew what a really good strawberry tasted like and would not compromise. In order to make sure that he had sufficient ripe peaches for his pies, he negotiated with a local orchard to ensure that they waited for all the peaches to be ripe before harvesting, offering to pay for any resulting product loss. He couldn't fathom how anyone could make a pie with inferior fruit or a leathery crust and have the nerve or cluelessness to put it on a menu.

After being in business for about sixteen years, my parents returned to farming once again while simultaneously shifting their focus from wholesale to direct-to-customer sales. As far as they were concerned, the best way to ensure a steady supply of quality produce for their pies was to grow it themselves, and the best way to sell the pies was to do it on their own terms. Thus, I spent the warm seasons of my adolescence working on the farm, mostly picking berries, and the cool seasons selling pies in the shop. (The first year we had the farm, before my parents bought a tractor, my siblings and I planted sixteen acres of pumpkins by hand—an experience that I will one day share with my own kids in a "when I was your age" rant.) In addition to the vegetables they grow for their farm share program, my family grows strawberries, raspberries, blackberries, rhubarb, sweet potatoes, and pumpkins, all for their pies. As you might expect, this has instilled in me both a high respect for farmers and uncompromising standards for flavorful produce.

Growing up in a family business has great benefits; it can make a family very cohesive, proud, and supportive of each other. At the same time, the idea that at some point the parents will one day pass the torch to their children, and the pressure that comes with it, lurks in the background. My siblings and I were always encouraged to explore our talents and get an education, but at certain points it was clear that my parents couldn't imagine any other alternative than for at least one of their four kids to take over the business.

Mom's Apple Pie Company is still going strong. My parents don't know how to retire, and two of my siblings, my brother Tyson and sister Ansa, are both heavily involved in the daily business operations. I, however, did something sort of odd. After I worked a number of years as a special education teacher in New York City public schools, my husband Robert and I decided to open our own pie shop in downtown Manhattan—an idea we conceived after just a couple months of dating. In doing so, I took the highest values of pie that I learned from my upbringing—both material and metaphorical—and set out to make damn fine pie for the damn fine people of New York City. I use more butter and less sugar than my dad, and some of my pies are a little

more adventurous, but the same thing drives us: We want to use real, simple ingredients to make you the best pie you've ever had.

We started with a shoestring budget; the bulk of our funds was money that Robert had won playing poker online and on weekend trips to Atlantic City. Over the course of three months I tested recipes in our apartment kitchen while we transformed a dingy pizzeria on Delancey Street into a tiny but efficient pie shop. My mom donated a two-thousand-pound dough mixer from the 1960s that she'd bought at an auction. We named our shop Petee's Pie Company (Petee was my childhood nickname) and opened for business two days before Thanksgiving in 2014. That first Thanksgiving we made one hundred pies. The following year I could be found mixing up one hundred pie–yield batches of pumpkin pie filling with our three-month-old daughter, Eloisa, strapped to my chest. We managed to make one thousand pies for our second Thanksgiving—at which point we realized we couldn't make as many pies as our customers demanded in such a tiny spot.

In 2018, we signed the lease for our second location in Clinton Hill, Brooklyn, two days before I gave birth to our son, Alejo. Four months later, I was once again wearing a baby while whipping up pies, although Alejo became too hefty too fast for me to keep wearing him to work. We named our second location Petee's Café and outfitted it with a great big kitchen and a beautiful fifteen-foot-long marble counter on which you can find about a dozen pie domes lined up on any given day. Our regulars, who spend hours sipping bottomless coffee and eating delicious biscuit sandwiches and pie, sometimes become a bit dismayed when Thanksgiving comes around and we have to transform their beloved neighborhood café into a veritable pie factory for a week. In 2019, five years in, we used all the power of that Brooklyn kitchen and all the might of our amazing bakers to make eight thousand pies during Thanksgiving week. I'm honored to share with you the recipes that have made Petee's such a beloved addition to the New York City food scene.

HOW TO USE THIS BOOK

In the next few pages, I give you foundational information

about my style of pie making and the standards by which I evaluate a pie. Before attempting to execute any of my recipes, I humbly ask that you read my advice for procuring ingredients, my guidance on the tools you will need, and instructions on how to properly measure and mix ingredients in order to make an outstanding pie.

The first chapter of recipes, "Crusts and Crumbs," gives you a number of pastry doughs and crumble toppings to choose from, as well as information on rolling dough, assembling pies, and decorative flourishes. The very first recipe in this book, my butter-crust pastry dough, is the one to master. However, I've included vegan, gluten-free, and whole-grain options as well. This allows you to make a pie using the crust and filling recipes that best suit the needs of you and your guests.

Four of the following chapters include recipes for pie fillings, both sweet and savory. Some recipes will include a specific crust or topping suggestion, but feel free to substitute based on preference or dietary needs. The remaining chapter includes recipes for ice cream and other toppings, from the classic vanilla ice cream to the more unusual but just as complementary cajeta, as well as suggested combinations for pie sundaes. In case learning how to make fabulous pies wasn't enough, the recipes in this chapter allow you to make multiple dessert presentations from the same pie.

One of the great benefits of sourcing ingredients the way I do is that I get a unique exposure to farmers and food purveyors. I realize that not everyone is so lucky! Interspersed with these recipes are accounts of my visits with farmers to give you an insight into why they do what they do and why their efforts are worth supporting. Additionally, I include some historical background on a few pies that enjoy a special status in our culinary history. My aim in writing this book is to share my pie-making expertise with you, as well as ground you in the notion that when you make a pie, you are participating in a timeless and meaningful culinary tradition and making it yours.

Rhubarb Pie with Brown
Butter Hazelnut-Almond
Streusel and Custard Sauce

PIE FOUNDATIONS

PIE STANDARDS

There are hundreds of ways to make a pie,

and just as many ways to evaluate one. My standards are heavily influenced by my father and were developed through various investigations—in the pie factory where I spent my formative years, at countless bakeries and restaurants, and in my own kitchens. Flavor and texture will trump presentation and innovation (or rather, gimmicks disguised as such) every damn time. Here are the tenets of good pie—the kind of pie you won't want to stop eating—that I'd like to pass on to you:

Crust should be flavorful and plastic-fork tender. For me, the standard bearer is a delicate butter crust made with not only good butter, but also fresh flour. Now that I have found excellent local sources of flour for my own bakery, I'm more sensitive to flour freshness and can tell by its smell whether it was milled recently or months ago.

Fruit fillings should be juicy, never dry. The raw fruit used in pie filling must be ripe and vibrant on its own, and its natural acidity and sweetness should be amplified with lemon juice and a modest amount of sugar.

Use spices wisely—the flavor should be subtle but perceptible. Most types of fruit pies don't benefit from the addition of spices, but tree fruits like apples, peaches, and pears can be enhanced by warm spices, such as cinnamon and nutmeg. Granted, this is a matter of personal opinion, but there's also a historical precedent for this concept. In Amelia Simmons's *American Cookery*, the first book ever published on the subject, she advises adding cinnamon and mace to apple pie but warns that "every species of fruit such as . . . plums, raspberries, black berries [sic] may be only sweetened, without spices." Defy this suggestion at your own peril.

Chess, nut, and **custard** pies can be as simple or elaborate as you like, but they need character beyond their richness and sweetness. Using fresh cream, high-quality vanilla, and flavorful sweeteners like apple blossom honey or maple syrup and browning the butter are all ways of adding character and depth of flavor.

Filling flavors must be balanced and harmonious. Never forgo salt. Don't combine elements merely based on how they sound or look together, but rather on the relationship between their respective flavors and textures.

Some of my favorite pies include (clockwise from top) Lemon Poppyseed Meringue, Brown Butter Honey Pecan, Key Lime with Vanilla Sea Salt Meringue, Sour Cherry with lattice crust, Chocolate Cream, and Lemon Chess.

Summer fruits of the Northeast, clockwise from above left: red and black currants, wild blueberries, and sour cherries

When sourcing ingredients

for pies, whether for Petee's or in my kitchen at home, I abide by the same general rule: Keep it local, seasonal, and/or very special. Any combination of these descriptors can be applied to the majority of the ingredients I use. If you are in a position to do the same, by engaging thoughtfully with the food at your local farmers' market, at your neighborhood grocery store, and even in some of the wild spaces hidden in plain sight, you will get an even greater satisfaction from your pie-making endeavors.

Year-round local

At Petee's, we buy anything that can be procured from farms located within a few hours of New York City. Most of our ingredients fit into this category. For example, we buy flour from Champlain Valley Milling; milk, cream, and butter from grass-fed cows from Kriemhild Dairy and Ronnybrook Dairy Farms; and free-range eggs from a number of upstate farms. There are a few local fruits that we use year-round or in their off season: frozen black currants from CurrantC Farm and frozen sour cherries and stored apples from Samascott Orchards.

There are several reasons that I am willing to pay twice as much or even more for a product grown by a local farmer, as opposed to buying mass-market products. The food miles are shorter, the quality is usually higher, and despite the higher cost, none of these farmers are getting rich. You know who is? The owners of large food companies who sell cheaper food of inferior quality. I'll be damned if I make them any richer!

Local and seasonal

There are some fruits and produce that grow locally, which I'll only use in season—mostly rhubarb, berries, and stone fruit. In our region, farmers don't do a lot of processing and freezing of these fruits because they have sufficient consumer demand within the window of seasonal availability, and as such they are able to sell most of their crop at peak ripeness.

To me, there is nothing tastier than a bright red strawberry or juicy nectarine eaten shortly after it's been picked. These fruits can be grown in many corners of the country, but it's an insult to compare the quality of a local berry eaten within its season to a "fresh" berry flown in from elsewhere. If I'm using frozen fruit, I'm doing it in part to support a local farmer. As such, you won't find us making strawberry-rhubarb pies in the dead of winter.

Seasonal and very special— but not local

For my purposes, this usually applies to citrus. Meyer lemons, pink grapefruit, and blood oranges are in season in California from autumn through early spring, but they can't be grown locally in my region. I won't turn up my nose at them because of that, however, because such a severe local-only orthodoxy would dampen my culinary creativity and joy! Using these fruits in season, even if their journey is a longer one, is like inviting some California sunshine into your kitchen.

Very special, but not local

If an ingredient isn't local *or* seasonal, it should be very special—and when you are thoughtful about your sourcing, even basic ingredients can be very special.

Some ingredients are very special by virtue of the fact that they grow only in particular climates and possess an inimitable flavor that aids in making unforgettable pies. Some of these are ubiquitous to the point that they seem ordinary, but they come from plants that are truly magical when you take the time to consider them—for example, chocolate, vanilla, coffee, and all manner of spices.

Other ingredients are very special because they fulfill an important culinary function (such as sugar for sweetening, lemon for acidity, or tapioca starch for thickening), or because they are crucial to the pie canon (such as the pecans in a pecan pie, the bananas in a banana cream pie, and the coconut in coconut custard).

Part of making these commonplace ingredients special is using the most responsibly produced versions I can find, which are often higher quality as well. For example, using fair-trade organic evaporated cane juice instead of cheap white sugar means that I'm not supporting farms where workers are exposed to pesticides that adversely affect their health, and also that, due to less processing, the trace minerals are intact, which gives the sugar a subtle, pleasant cane flavor. In my experience, I've found that organic fair-trade spices tend to be more potent and vibrant, and thus less is needed to flavor a pie. It's also possible to get some of these ingredients from local producers who source thoughtfully, even if they come from plants that are grown out of your reach—such as coffee from a local roaster and chocolate from a local bean-to-bar purveyor.

Local, seasonal, and very special

This category is my favorite because it includes the ingredients that truly ground you in a sense of time and place. For me, this includes all sorts of foraged foods, from fiddlehead ferns to black walnuts to juneberries, as well as heirloom varieties of fruits and vegetables that are only grown by farmers who take a special interest in such things.

When you forage for your own food, whether in Central Park or Appalachia, or make food with plants that someone has foraged for you, you are engaging with your food in the most profound way possible. You are connecting and delighting with the Earth and all her abundance, as directly as you can. Making a pie with foraged fruit and sharing it with someone is a genuine expression of love.

A late summer haul from my parents' farm includes lima beans and all manner of gourds (clockwise from top right): Carolina candy roaster squash, neck pumpkin, Porcelain Doll pumpkin, and Blue Hubbard squash

Gorgeous yellow peaches from New Jersey that we blanch and peel by the bushel for our pies.

A farmer's ardor for heirloom fruit is also undeniable. Most of the small farmers I know are scientists and naturalists in their own right, constantly observing the natural world, experimenting, and deepening their relationship to the plants they grow. They are delighted by the bountiful diversity of apples, tomatoes, beans, and corn at their disposal, and they are determined to do their part to grow them well and share them with you. When you meet them at a market and use their produce, you are bringing their vision to fruition.

A note on frozen fruit

Don't be afraid to cook with frozen fruit! In fact, if you're dying to make a pie from fruit that is not in season locally, frozen fruit is superior to fruit that has been transported from elsewhere. Why? First, if a fruit is going to be cooked in the oven, the texture will be changed so drastically that it doesn't matter if it's been frozen first. Second, the so-called fresh fruit that you can find out of season in the grocery store doesn't taste as good as fruit that was frozen when it was ripe. This is either (1) because they are fruit cultivars chosen solely for their ability to withstand travel, like the sturdy, insipid strawberries with white cores you find in grocery stores under a brand name I will not mention here, or (2) because the fruit is harvested

while still unripe in order to withstand travel, like the dry, pithy peaches with no acidity to speak of that are imported from South America so that you can buy them at the grocery store in December.

For some farmers, it's virtually impossible to disperse their product to enough sales outlets to sell all of their fruit fresh. Instead, they freeze some or all of it at peak ripeness, often on the same day it is picked. This allows commercial bakers and home cooks alike to use it many months later, while reaping the same gastronomic and health benefits of fresh, seasonal fruit. IQF (individually quick frozen) fruit works well in the recipes in this book, because there is no added sugar to throw off the proportions.

If you have a local farmers' market, ask your farmers if they sell frozen fruit in the off season. Otherwise, organic frozen fruit from the grocery store is usually high quality. Avoid frozen fruit that contains sugar, which would throw off the ratios in your recipe.

You can also freeze your own fruit by spreading it out on a baking sheet lined with wax paper and putting it in the freezer overnight. After it reaches a hard freeze, transfer it to an airtight container. Break it out of the freezer in the middle of winter, when you're dying for a taste of summer, or store it up to eighteen months.

Here are a few things that make pie making easier and more efficient:

Scale A small digital kitchen scale that measures in grams is preferred. This is crucial because volume is not a reliable way to measure ingredients such as flour or fruit.

Pie baking vessels Unless otherwise noted, the recipes in this book are intended to be made in a pie pan that is approximately 9 inches (23 cm) across and 1 to 1¼ inches (2.5 to 3 cm) deep. Anything from a recyclable aluminum pie tin to a handmade ceramic pie dish will do. Clear glass dishes are inexpensive, great at conducting heat, and as a bonus, it's easy to see if your crust has cooked through. A word of advice—avoid glass and ceramic dishes with wavy or crimped edges, which can make it harder to remove a slice of pie with a delicate crust.

Rolling pin A simple, old-fashioned wood rolling pin is fine, but there are other options out there. Marble rolling pins are pretty neat—they can be chilled before use, so they're very handy for warmer seasons if it's hard to keep your kitchen cool.

Rolling pin bands or dowels These are optional, but they're very helpful for the pastry novice for ensuring that your dough is rolled to an even thickness. The bands can be found at kitchen specialty shops and put around both ends of the roller to ensure that the dough cannot be rolled beyond the thickness of the bands. Dowels, which can be purchased at a hardware store, are set on either side of your dough mound, with the distance between them being slightly less than the length of the roller. Roll the dough with the rolling pin directly on the dowels, sort of like a train track, to make sure that the dough is rolled no thinner than the dowels. Typically, you'll want to roll your dough between ⅛ inch (3 mm) thick and ¼ inch (6 mm) thick. With dowels, choose a set, or a few pairs, that fall within this range. Rolling pin bands are often sold in sets of various thicknesses.

Silicone mat Silicone mats take up barely any space, which I appreciate in my Brooklyn apartment's tiny kitchen. I like to roll dough on a silicone mat because it makes cleaning up that much easier. Since they are flexible, they can also be used to transfer the rolled dough onto your pie vessel.

Blender A standard blender or immersion blender can be used to mix a variety of pie fillings, although most can be mixed by hand. An immersion blender has the added benefit of being suitable to mix ingredients right in a mixing bowl or even in a saucepan on the stove.

Electric mixer Stand mixers are the most convenient for handling tasks such as making meringue. Hand mixers can get the job done, too, albeit with a little more work on your part.

Food processor While this isn't required for most recipes, certain tasks are almost impossible without a food processor—for example, the chestnut puree for Nesselrode Pies (page 136) would be hard to make any other way. You can also make a crumb-bottom crust or topping in the food processor quickly and conveniently.

Flexible rubber spatula The portions in my fillings are exact, so I advise using a rubber spatula to get every last drop from your mixing bowl.

Pastry bag with large plain and fluted tips
These can be filled with whipped cream or meringue, which you can then apply to the top of chilled pies.

Multiwheel pastry cutter This isn't really necessary unless you want to make a lot of lattice-top pies, but it's very fun to use!

Fluted pastry cutter For making fancy ruffled edges on your lattice.

Pastry brush For gently applying egg wash.

Candy thermometer This is necessary for ensuring the proper setting of precooked fillings and the appropriate temperature for the sugar syrup used in Italian meringue.

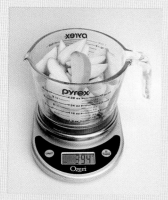

There are enough variables

in pie making to warrant its reputation for being tricky and hard to master. However, controlling those variables by using a consistent method of measurement for certain ingredients—fruit and flour, specifically—will help you make excellent pies every time. Here's what you need to know:

Liquid measurements will be quantified in cups and teaspoons/tablespoons as well as milliliters.

Flour can have drastically different weights per cup, depending on how compressed it is in the cup. If you don't have a kitchen scale, you must measure your flour by a particular method. Do not compress the flour into your measuring cup before leveling it off. Instead, scoop small spoonfuls of flour into the measuring cup, then level it off by scraping the flat side of a knife over the edge of the cup. Flour quantities will be listed both by cups and by weight in grams—I recommend you use the grams.

Eggs, for the purposes of these recipes, are large eggs. An egg white is a white from a large egg, and an egg yolk is a yolk from a large egg. Whenever a specific measurement of yolks or whites is crucial to the success of a recipe, a liquid measurement may be included as well.

Fruit can also have different weights per cup, depending on its water content and the size of the fruit pieces, which are crucial factors in determining how runny or congealed the filling will be in the finished product. Fruit quantities will be listed both by cups and by weight in grams—I recommend you use the grams.

Look closely at the numbers on the scale. Flour that is compacted into a measuring cup (top) can weigh 25 percent more than flour that is measured with a light touch (second from top). Fruit that takes up the same amount of space (second from bottom and left) can have very different weights depending on its size, shape, and water content.

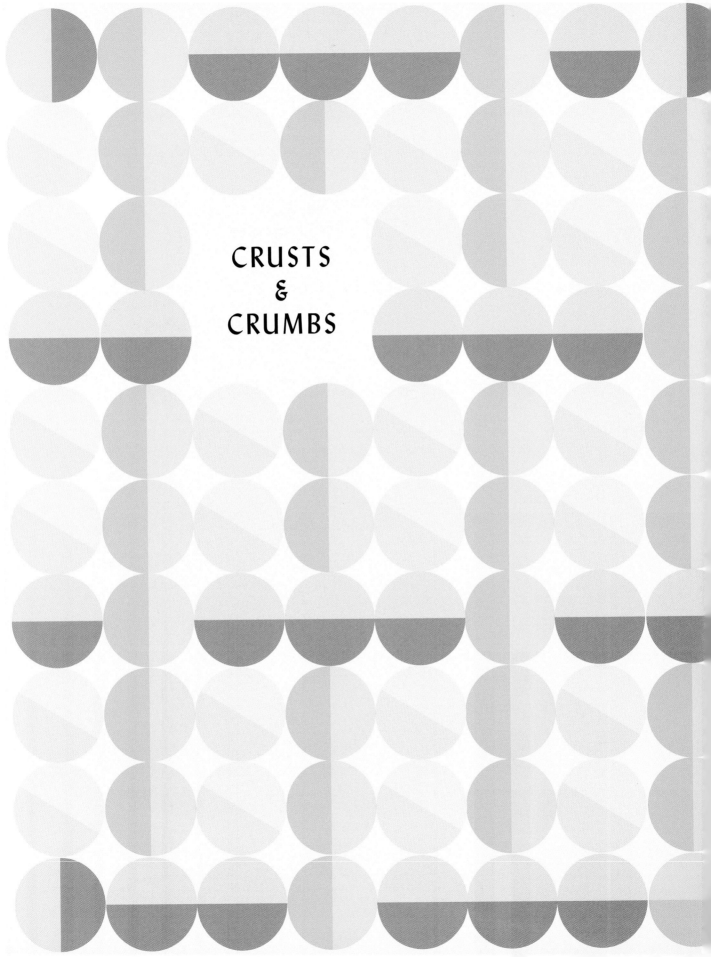

CRUSTS
&
CRUMBS

Even experienced bakers can get a little clammy at the idea of having to make a pie crust, because there are so many ways for a pie crust to be wrong. Among the adjectives we don't want to hear in reference to crust are: pasty, mealy, doughy, tough, and bland.

However, pie eaters are willing to forgive a range of mild structural transgressions, such as a fruit pie that settles on the plate rather than standing at attention, or the crimped edge breaking away from a custard pie, as long as you present them with a crust that is crisp, rich, flaky, and tender. The following recipes—whether you choose the classic butter crust or opt for a gluten-free or vegan option—all use fat, flour, and water in the correct proportions and at the right temperature to achieve this goal.

While my pastry dough methods may seem different, after the first try you'll realize how easy it can be to make a life-changing pie crust. You might even get in the habit of stocking up on pastry dough in the freezer (see page 61) so that you can whip up a pie in a snap whenever the inspiration strikes you.

In addition to the pastry dough, there are a variety of crumb and streusel options that you can use to top fruit pies. The aim is versatility, so you can make multiple versions of the same pie, depending on your personal tastes and needs. Are your vegan niece and your gluten-eschewing neighbor joining you for Thanksgiving, and everyone expects apple pie? Do you have a bumper crop of rhubarb at your disposal? Perhaps you got in over your head at a pick-your-own berry farm? There are dozens of crust and crumb combinations you can make with any of the fruit fillings in this book, and a handful of crust options for most of the other fillings as well.

Additionally, I will teach you how to successfully roll out pastry dough, assemble double-crust pies, weave a lattice crust, and crimp the edge of a pie. The methods you learn here will transform pie making from a daunting task into a second-nature skill. Let's break out the butter and get rolling!

AN ODE TO BUTTER CRUST

There are generally three fat options when it comes to pie crust: vegetable shortening, animal fat, or butter. Pie makers tend to have strong opinions on which is best. The main considerations are ease of use and the flavor and texture of the finished product. Butter has the reputation for being the most difficult to work with, which might make a baker wonder if it's worthwhile to make a butter crust.

For some bakers, vegetable shortening is a viable option. It is pure fat that is solid at room temperature, it's usually vegan, and it makes a tender dough that is perhaps the easiest to work with. That said, it does have its pitfalls. The main drawbacks for me are that vegetable shortening is far removed from nature, not to mention completely devoid of flavor—you won't find it in my recipes.

Other pie makers swear by rendered animal fat, most commonly lard, but sometimes even beef tallow. It shares the same properties as vegetable shortening, so it's easy to work with, but it has a meaty richness that some folks crave. I do find a lard crust conceptually appealing, as it aligns with a more ethical "whole animal" approach to omnivorism. I include a recipe for lard crust because the idea of a tart apple filling contrasted with a rich, animal-inflected crust really is lovely, and it also works well for savory pies. Still, it isn't my go-to. I tend to enjoy large servings of pie, so most of the time lard is simply too rich for me.

Different people value different things, and we live in a highly visual age. It's okay to want a beautiful pie with ornate crimpwork, and to take pictures of said pie. However, if you plan on serving your pie to people you

Cracks in the crust, while
an optical imperfection,
are a sign that a crust is
tender, rather than tough
and overworked.

care about, or whom you at least want to impress, you should probably concern yourself with the most important question of all: How does it taste? I want to eat pie crust that tastes like what it's made from, and butter tastes best.

There are some aesthetic concessions you make when you make a pie with an extremely buttery crust. It will be delicate. The filling may bubble up and crack the crust. You definitely can't send it in the mail because the crust will crumble to bits. Fruit pies with especially juicy fillings (peach or strawberry-rhubarb, for example) won't always hold their shape when sliced and plated. Once you taste a perfectly delicious butter crust, though, none of that will matter.

One of the culinary accomplishments I'm most proud of is the amount of butter I've worked into my recipe. When we first started Petee's I used my dad's crust recipe, which made a lovely, buttery crust. But once I got comfortable as a professional pie maker, and when our business was on solid enough footing to bear a $415 experiment, I decided it was time to see if I could take it a little further. My goal was to create a shockingly good crust—one that shattered like butter suspended by just enough flour. I put the usual seventy-five pounds of pastry flour in my decades-old Artofex dough mixer along with the usual fifty-pound block of grass-fed butter. Then

I added an additional seventeen pounds of butter—about 33 percent more. With a few adjustments—specifically, substituting some all-purpose for a portion of the pastry flour to provide a little more structure—I was able to sufficiently differentiate my recipe from my dad's and make a crust that surprised and delighted even those who thought they didn't like pie.

Done right, a butter crust is delicate, tender, and rich in a sweet, clean way. It is equally adaptable to sweet and savory dishes. That said, many butter crust recipes won't get you this result, so I can't blame any baker for trying and giving up on butter crust. Butter transforms swiftly from solid and cold to soft and greasy right on your fingertips. When preparing dough, the goal is to encapsulate small pieces of fat in flour before adding liquid, which creates flaky layers. Since it emulsifies so easily, using butter can make this tricky—but it can be done! One of the keys to butter crust success (and one that is often left out of recipes) is managing the temperature of all your ingredients. If you are using cold butter and water but your flour is straight out of the cabinet in your warm kitchen, you're going to have a hell of a time keeping the butter cool enough to prevent excessive emulsification. But if your cold butter is surrounded by flour from the freezer, it will be protected from the heat of your hands and a warm ambient temperature.

Another challenging aspect of butter is that it has a lower percentage of fat and a higher water content than shortening or lard. This means that you need to use less water to form the dough, and this is where even professional bakers go wrong. Some tout the importance of using "European-style" butter, due to its higher fat and lower water content. But right after administering this advice, they go on to instruct you to add about twice as much water as my recipe requires. Excessive water overdevelops the gluten in the flour, both toughening the crust and diminishing the flavor of the butter. If it's tough for your fork to break through, it's going to be tough for your teeth, too.

A poorly executed butter crust turns dull and tough, or it becomes simply impossible to work with. This is why people may turn to tricks like replacing some of the water with vodka or vinegar, but you won't find those drastic measures here. I've developed simple, foolproof methods to achieve a succulent butter crust every time. Once you try them, you'll never look back.

SEVEN TYPES OF PIE CRUST

*Each recipe yields enough dough to make two bottom crusts or
one double-crust pie*

THE FOLLOWING SEVEN DOUGHS GIVE YOU THE OPPORTUNITY
to make pies to accommodate a variety of diets and preferences,
because everyone should be able to partake in the pleasures of
a homemade pie. To successfully execute these recipes it is crucial
to keep the ingredients at the right temperature, which allows
you to incorporate the fat into the flour without emulsifying it.
Unless otherwise noted, an ingredient should be room temperature
(68 to 72°F/20 to 22°C). Depending on the type of pastry dough you
are making, an ingredient may be specified as "cold," which would
be in the fridge range of 34 to 40°F (1 to 4°C), or freezer temperature,
which is below 30°F (−1°C). My unusual technique of dissolving
the sugar and salt in water, rather than adding them to the flour,
ensures even seasoning for a flavorful dough.

See pages 41–47 for instructions for three different methods for
making dough.

BUTTER PASTRY DOUGH

It's abundantly clear that I have a passion for
butter crust, and if you only use one of my
pastry dough recipes, I hope it is my butter
pastry dough.

1 tablespoon sugar

1¼ teaspoons salt

¼ cup (60 ml) boiling water

**1½ loosely filled cups (180 g) pastry
flour, from the freezer**

**⅔ loosely filled cup (80 g) all-purpose
flour, from the freezer**

**1 cup (2 sticks/225 g) cold unsalted
butter, cut into ½-inch (12-mm) pieces**

Extra flour, for rolling

VEGAN PASTRY DOUGH

Instead of vegan shortenings with long lists of ingredients and stabilizers, I prefer to use coconut oil. If you don't mind a distinct coconut flavor, you can use unrefined coconut oil in this recipe, which is nutritionally superior. Otherwise, use refined coconut oil, which won't impart a noticeable coconut flavor.

4 teaspoons sugar

1½ teaspoons salt

¼ cup plus 2 tablespoons (90 ml) boiling water

2¼ loosely filled cups (250 g) pastry flour, from the freezer

7 ounces (200 g) room-temperature (solid) refined coconut oil, divided into teaspoon-size pieces

Extra flour, for rolling

CORN PASTRY DOUGH

Corn doesn't contain any gluten, so the bread flour makes up for that in order to make a more cohesive dough. The distinctly corny flavor works well as a stand-in for tamal masa or tortillas in the Chile Verde Pork Pie (page 204). It's also great with summer fruit pies such as peach (page 72).

1 tablespoon sugar

1¼ teaspoons salt

⅓ cup (75 ml) boiling water

2 loosely filled cups (225 g) corn flour (not to be confused with cornstarch)

¼ loosely filled cup (35 g) bread flour

1 cup (2 sticks/225 g) cold unsalted butter, cut into ½-inch (12-mm) pieces

Extra corn or wheat flour, for rolling

GLUTEN-FREE PASTRY DOUGH

This recipe is suitable for those who are avoiding gluten by choice or necessity. For a pie to be truly gluten-free, it is important to make sure your preparation area is completely free of flour, to ensure that you use only gluten-free oat flour, and to verify that any flavorings you use in the filling, such as vanilla extract, are gluten-free as well.

1 tablespoon sugar

1¼ teaspoons salt

¼ cup (60 ml) boiling water

1 loosely filled cup (90 g) gluten-free oat flour

½ loosely filled cup (60 g) brown rice flour

⅓ cup (60 g) sweet rice flour

⅓ cup (40 g) cassava flour

1 cup (2 sticks/225 g) cold unsalted butter, cut into ½-inch (12-mm) pieces

Extra flour (any of the above), for rolling

RYE PASTRY DOUGH

Rye flour isn't gluten-free, but it contains less gluten than wheat flour. In order to make up for that and help the dough come together, this recipe contains a small amount of bread flour. Use the rye pastry dough to impart an earthy, nutty flavor to a savory pie.

1 tablespoon sugar

1¼ teaspoons salt

⅓ cup (75 ml) boiling water

2¾ loosely filled cups (225 g) rye flour

¼ loosely filled cup (35 g) bread flour

1 cup (2 sticks/225 g) cold unsalted butter, cut into ½-inch (12-mm) pieces

Extra rye or wheat flour, for rolling

LARD PASTRY DOUGH

This recipe is ideal for savory pies, where you can counterbalance its richness with a brightly dressed salad or slaw. It also makes an interesting contrast to a tart apple filling.

2½ teaspoons sugar

1¼ teaspoons salt

¼ cup plus 2 tablespoons (90 ml) boiling water

2¼ loosely filled cups (270 g) pastry flour

7 ounces (200 g) cold leaf lard, cut into ½-inch (12-mm) pieces

Extra flour, for rolling

WHOLE-WHEAT PASTRY DOUGH

While pastry and all-purpose flours are made with wheat from which the bran has been removed, whole-wheat flour is made from intact wheat kernels. This means that the fiber, oils, and nutrients contained in the bran all make their way into the flour. Whole-wheat flour makes dough that is dense and crispy compared to one made with pastry or all-purpose flour. It makes a very wholesome quiche shell and works well with pumpkin and sweet potato pies.

1 tablespoon sugar

1¼ teaspoons salt

¼ cup (60 ml) boiling water

2¼ loosely filled cups (280 g) whole-wheat or graham flour

1 cup (2 sticks/225 g) cold unsalted butter, cut into ½-inch (12-mm) pieces

Extra flour, for rolling

THREE METHODS OF MAKING DOUGH

HERE ARE MY THREE RECOMMENDED WAYS TO MAKE DOUGH.
All three will work with any dough type (except vegan dough
shouldn't be made with the grating method). Which you choose
will depend on what equipment you have available and your own
personal preference. If you are new to pie baking, I recommend
you start with making the dough by hand, so that you can feel the
dough come together, and then experiment with the other methods to find your favorite.

MAKING DOUGH BY HAND

I LIKE MAKING DOUGH BY HAND BECAUSE FEELING THE DOUGH
gives me valuable feedback—whether there are still any large chunks
of fat that need to be broken down, for instance, or if the dough is
getting too warm or sticky and I need to put it in the fridge for a few
minutes. Whenever I teach this method of making dough, pie stu-
dents start getting nervous about halfway through. It seems like the
flour and butter won't cohere into a dough, but I tell them to resist
the urge to add more water. Instead, compressing the dough swiftly
and repeatedly forces it to stick together. For this reason, having faith
in the method is just as important as using the right ingredients.

Stir the sugar, salt, and water together in a small bowl until the sugar
and salt are fully dissolved. Place the bowl in the freezer—the liquid
needs to be ice cold before it is added to the dough.

(1) Put the flour(s) in a large bowl and dump the butter, lard, or
coconut oil into the flour. Toss to coat the pieces of fat in the flour.
Working quickly, (2) use your thumbs and index fingers to squeeze
each chunk of fat into a thin sheet, between ⅛ and ¼ inch (3 and
6 mm) thick. Shake the contents of the bowl (3) to ensure the sheets
are well-coated in flour.

(4) Sprinkle the ice-cold sugar-salt solution over the fat and flour.
(5) Use your fingers to lightly toss the contents of the bowl around to
disperse the liquid.

(6, 7) Squeeze the shaggy mess with your fists, repeatedly and
quickly, until the chunks get bigger and more cohesive.

(8) At first it will be crumbly and seem as if it won't come together,
but with continued compression, you can begin to make two
mounds of dough of roughly equal size. (9) Flatten your mounds into
1-inch- (2.5-cm-) thick disks.

See page 50 for instructions on rolling your dough.

MAKING DOUGH WITH A GRATER

I'VE ALWAYS FOUND PASTRY CUTTERS TO BE CUMBERSOME— the dull edges never seem to be as effective as I'd like, and too much dough gets caught between the blades as you go. A grater—left in the freezer for 15 minutes before using so it doesn't melt the fat on contact—works as a great alternative, because it makes uniformly small pieces of fat that you then disperse throughout the flour. Make sure that you freeze your butter or lard before grating; otherwise they'll turn into mush on the grater. This method isn't recommended for the vegan dough because the coconut oil liquefies too easily.

Stir the sugar, salt, and water together in a small bowl until the sugar and salt are fully dissolved. Place the bowl in the freezer—the liquid needs to be ice cold before it is added to the dough.

Put the flour(s) in a large bowl. Position the grater directly over the bowl. (1) Grate the butter or lard right into the flour, shaking the bowl every so often to coat the fat in flour. Make sure you don't leave any of the fat inside the grater. (2) Toss to fully coat the pieces of fat in flour.

(3) Sprinkle the ice-cold sugar-salt solution over the fat and flour. (4) Use your fingers to lightly toss the contents of the bowl around to disperse the liquid.

(5, 6, 7) Squeeze the shaggy mess with your fists, repeatedly and quickly, until the chunks get bigger and more cohesive.

(8, 9, 10) At first it will be crumbly and seem as if it won't come together, but with continued compression, you can begin to make two mounds of dough of roughly equal size. (11, 12) Flatten your mounds into 1-inch- (2.5-cm-) thick disks.

See page 50 for instructions on rolling your dough.

MAKING DOUGH IN A FOOD PROCESSOR

IF YOU HAVE A LARGE-CAPACITY FOOD PROCESSOR, IT'S A GREAT tool for making pastry dough. A standard food processor can be used for a full recipe while a smaller food processor can handle a half batch. In this method, the fat is added in two stages. The first fat addition will be more integrated into the flour by the end, which helps the flour become resistant to the water, preventing the overdevelopment of gluten. The second addition of fat allows some of the fat to remain in larger pieces, creating a flaky dough. (This process happens naturally when you're making dough by hand.)

Stir the sugar, salt, and water together in a small bowl until the sugar and salt are fully dissolved. Place the bowl in the freezer—the liquid needs to be ice cold before it is added to the dough.

(1) Put the flour(s) in the bowl of a food processor and add half of the fat. Pulse until the fat is in pea-size pieces.

(2, 3) Add the remaining fat and sprinkle the ice-cold sugar-salt solution over the fat and flour. Pulse a few more times, until the newly added fat pieces are pea-size. The mixture will still be crumbly—resist the temptation to process it into a consistent mass.

(4, 5) Dump the contents of the bowl onto a silicone mat dusted with flour. Dust your hands with flour and use them to compress the crumbly dough into two 1-inch- (2.5-cm-) thick disks of roughly equal size.

See page 50 for instructions on rolling your dough.

CRUST FLAVOR VARIATIONS

ONCE YOU MASTER THE PASTRY DOUGH OF YOUR CHOICE, YOU can play around with additions that offer variety and texture. Since they add a little crunch and flavor, they work particularly well for simple chess pies, as well as chilled pies that use blind-baked bottom crusts.

COCONUT CRUST VARIATION FOR CHILLED PIES

This one is best for blind-baking for icebox pies. It doesn't work as well for pies that need to be baked, since it contains additional sugar that would cause it to burn before the filling cooks fully.

To the dough recipe of your choice (see pages 38–40), add 1 cup (85 g) unsweetened shredded coconut and ¼ cup (50 g) sugar, tossing to disperse through the dough before squeezing the dough with your fists, or if using the food processor method, while forming the dough into disks. This dough is very likely to break when transferring it into a pan, so use a silicone mat to help you transfer. Use your fingers to gently press the dough back together if it breaks when you transfer it into the pan.

SEEDED CRUST VARIATION

To the dough recipe of your choice (see pages 38–40), add 2 tablespoons poppyseeds, white sesame seeds, or black sesame seeds, tossing to disperse through the dough before squeezing the dough with your fists.

NUTTY CRUST VARIATION

To the dough recipe of your choice (see pages 38–40), add ⅔ cup (55 g) nut meal or ground nuts (almond, pistachio, and hazelnut are all great options), tossing to disperse through the dough, after dispersing the liquid but before compressing the dough with your fists. This dough is very likely to break when transferring it into a pan, so use a silicone mat to help you transfer. Use your fingers to gently press the dough back together if it breaks when you transfer it into the pan.

WORKING WITH THE DOUGH

ONCE YOU'VE MADE YOUR DOUGH, THERE ARE A FEW DIFFERENT directions you can go, but they all start with rolling. The recipes all yield enough dough to make both a top and bottom crust or two bottom crusts, plus a little extra to bake into a sweet snack I call Sugar Scraps (page 63).

If your kitchen is warm and the dough feels soft, you may want to chill your dough for 15 to 20 minutes before rolling. Alternatively, if it feels chilly and stiff, leave it to rest at room temperature for around 20 minutes before rolling. Due to the low moisture and high fat content of these doughs, there's very little gluten development. This means that if the dough is at room temperature, there's no need to let it rest for an hour before rolling it, as per standard pastry wisdom. With the exception of a few of the savory pies, you will need to start by making a bottom crust.

HOW TO ROLL A DOUGH SHEET
AND MAKE A BOTTOM CRUST

Prepare a clean, dry, nonporous surface by sprinkling it with the flour appropriate for your choice of dough.

(1) Place a disk of dough on top of the floured surface and sprinkle it with a little more flour. Place your rolling pin in the center of the dough and roll away from yourself with firm, even pressure, but not enough force to squish the dough. As you approach the edge of the dough, use a little less pressure so that it doesn't become too thin on the edges.

(2) Rotate the dough about 45 degrees. Place the rolling pin at the center of the disk and roll away from yourself once again.

(3) Continue to rotate and roll, adding more flour as needed to prevent the dough from sticking to the surface and/or the rolling pin, (4) until you've rolled the dough to approximately ⅛ inch (3 mm) thick. If the dough starts to split on the edges, you can gently press it back together before continuing to roll it out. The finished sheet of dough should be roughly 12 inches (30.5 cm) in diameter.

(5, 6) Transfer the sheet of dough into a pie pan, centering it so that you have at least 1 inch (2.5 cm) of extra dough all the way around the edges of the pan. While transferring, support the dough with your fingers spread out, in order to distribute the weight and prevent breakage.

Alternatively, put your hand and wrist under the silicone mat along the center line of the dough circle and pick it up, letting one half of the circle hang on one side of your hand, and the other half of the dough circle hang on the other side.

Lay one half of the dough along the center line of the pie pan, then fold the other half over so the silicone mat is lying over the top, then remove the mat.

(7, 8) Once the sheet of dough is in the pan, ease it into the corner where the base of the pan meets the sides.

In order to do this without stretching or breaking the dough, lift the edge of the dough with one hand to allow it to fall into place while gently pressing it into the corner with the other. (9) If not crimping or adding a top crust, trim the crust by running a knife all the way around the outer edge of the pan.

HOW TO MAKE A CRIMPED BOTTOM SHELL

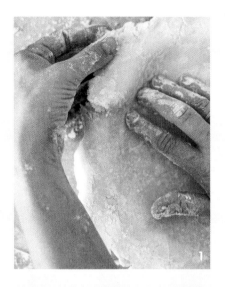

After transferring your dough sheet into the pie pan, **(1)** lift the edge of the dough up to make a raised, hollow area, about ⅜ inch (1 cm) or a little less than ½ inch (12 mm) high, over the edge of the pie pan, **(2)** pressing the excess dough against the rim of the pie pan to trim it. This will give you enough dough to form a decorative edge.

(3) Then position the thumb and forefinger of your nondominant hand so that there's about ½ inch (12 mm) of dough between them, and push them gently into the edge of the crust, right over the rim of the pie dish, while simultaneously using the forefinger of your dominant hand to push the dough from the opposite side into the space between your thumb and forefinger.

Shift your nondominant hand so that your thumb is now in the spot that your nondominant index finger just occupied, and repeat the same motion. Continue all the way around the edge of the pie. The rounded edges that result from this method prevent the burning that would otherwise happen if you pinched the dough into thin, sharp points.

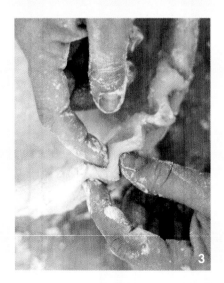

HOW TO ASSEMBLE A DOUBLE-CRUST PIE

A double-crust pie is one with a layer of crust on both the bottom and top. It's that simple! The style is usually used with fruit pies, but you can make double-crust savory pies as well (as opposed to a pot pie, which just has a layer of crust on the top). You can use any of the pastry dough recipes to make a double-crust pie.

After transferring your dough sheet into the pie pan, trim the bottom crust by running a knife all the way around the outer edge of the pan.

Fill the shell with the filling, and use a pastry brush to gently brush water around the rim of the bottom crust. (1) Roll a top crust in the same manner as the bottom and lay it over the filling. (2) Trim the top crust so that there is about ½ inch (12 mm) of extra dough all around the edge. (3) Lift the edge of the bottom crust up and tuck the extra top-crust dough underneath it.

Then, crimp in the same manner shown in photo 3 on page 52. Position the thumb and forefinger of your nondominant hand so that there's about ½ inch (12 mm) of dough between them, and push them gently into the edge of the crust, right over the rim of the pie dish, while simultaneously using the forefinger of your dominant hand to push the dough from the opposite side into the space between your thumb and forefinger.

Shift your nondominant hand so that your thumb is now in the spot that your index finger just occupied and repeat the same motion. Continue all the way around the edge of the pie. Before baking, brush the surface of the pie with an egg wash (see page 56), avoiding the crimped edges and taking care not to allow the egg wash to pool in any recessed areas. Use a sharp paring knife to cut vents into the top crust, which will help steam escape. Bake immediately.

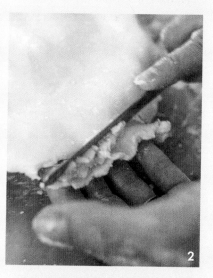

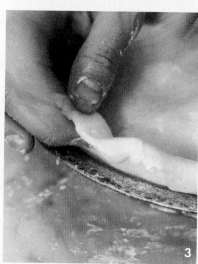

HOW TO ASSEMBLE A LATTICE CRUST PIE

Aside from looking pretty, lattice crusts allow a fruit filling to bubble and vent freely, which makes them perfect for juicier fillings, such as cherry, peach, and any other stone fruit, for that matter. Butter or lard pastry doughs are the easiest to use for a lattice crust, but with a little care you can make a vegan or gluten-free lattice crust as well. I don't recommend the whole-wheat, rye, or corn pastry doughs for lattices because they're more likely to break.

(1) After transferring your dough sheet into the pie pan, trim the bottom crust by running a knife all the way around the outer edge of the pan. Fill the shell with the filling, then use a pastry brush to gently brush water around the rim of the bottom crust. Incorporate the trimmings into your second disk of dough, then break that into two pieces. (2) Roll each piece into an oval about 10 inches (25 cm) long and 8 inches (20 cm) wide. One oval will make your vertical strips and the other will make your horizontal strips. Transfer the ovals onto wax paper and chill them in the fridge for about 10 minutes.

Cut five long strips lengthwise from each oval about 1½ inches (4 cm) wide. (If you wish, you can make more narrow strips or fewer wider strips and follow the same general instructions.)

(3) Place the longest center strip and the two outermost strips from one of the ovals vertically on the pie, leaving space between each strip to fit another strip. (4) Place the center strip from the other oval perpendicularly across them in the center.

(5) Place the two remaining strips from the vertical oval over the horizontal strip into the gaps you left earlier.

(6) Gently weave the center and outer strips down over the horizontal strip, and lay the next-longest horizontal strip down across the pie. Bring the center and outer strips back up. Bring the other two strips down and place a smaller horizontal strip across the pie, then bring all the strips back up.

(7) Repeat with the remaining horizontal strips on the other side of the center strip.

(8) Trim any excess off the strips around the edge of the pie, and gently press the strips onto the edge of the bottom crust. (9) Either crimp between your fingers as detailed on page 52, or use the tine of a fork or round edge of a butter knife to make an imprint in the crust and seal the top and bottom crusts together.

Before baking, brush the lattice crust with an egg wash (see page 56), avoiding the crimped edges. Bake immediately.

HOW TO MAKE AND APPLY AN EGG WASH

Makes enough to coat many pies

Egg wash gives fruit pies and savory pies a deep golden hue and pretty sheen. It also equalizes the color tone between the crimped edges of a double-crust pie and the crust that tops the filling.

1 egg

2 tablespoons sugar

In a small bowl, beat the egg and sugar with a whisk until smooth. Before baking, brush the surface of the pie(s) with the egg mixture, avoiding the crimped edges and taking care not to allow the egg wash to pool in any recessed areas. Discard any excess egg wash. Bake immediately.

VARIATION FOR VEGAN FRUIT PIES

Brush a small amount of maple syrup on the crust for a similar effect to an egg wash.

Make sure to add egg wash to your lattice-topped pies, which will make the crust brown beautifully. There are so many fun aesthetic variations to explore when you make a lattice crust pie. The strips can be narrow or wide, with a straight or crimped edge as shown here, created with a fluted pastry cutter. You can let a juicy filling peek through or keep it covered. The best part? You get almost double the buttery crust on top, with lots of crispy edges.

HOW TO MAKE A PIE WITH A CRUMB OR STREUSEL TOP

Each version makes enough crumb or streusel for one 9-inch (23-cm) pie

THE DIFFERENCE BETWEEN A CRUMB TOPPING AND A STREUSEL is simply that a crumb is made with cold butter that is broken into pieces, while a streusel is made with melted butter that is poured over the dry ingredients. Crumb- or streusel-topped pies have a little extra sweetness and crunch that goes really well with a fruit pie. The warm nuttiness and additional sweetness offer a pleasant contrast to the bright, tart filling of pies like a Sour Cherry or Black Currant (pages 76 and 82). Alternatively, a crumb topping can double down on the warm, autumnal flavors of a fall fruit like apple or pear. If you're using a full dough recipe but only making one pie with a bottom crust, you can make a second "shell" (my term for a rolled-and-ready bottom crust in a pie pan) to keep in the freezer (see page 61), or you can use the remaining dough for Sugar Scraps (page 63).

CORNMEAL·PECAN CRUMB

This recipe is based on my dad's crumb recipe. It adds a nutty sweetness and crunchy texture that complements any fruit filling, although I'm partial to pairing it with Sour Cherry (page 76) or Wild Blueberry (page 88). To make it vegan, use coconut oil instead of butter, and to make it gluten-free, substitute the all-purpose flour for gluten-free oat flour.

¼ **cup plus 2 tablespoons (70 g) cold corn flour or extra-fine cornmeal**

¼ **cup plus 2 tablespoons (45 g) cold all-purpose flour or gluten-free oat flour**

½ **cup (110 g) packed brown sugar**

½ **cup (1 stick/115 g) cold unsalted butter, or ½ cup (105 g) cold refined coconut oil, divided into teaspoon-size pieces**

½ **teaspoon vanilla**

⅓ **cup (40 g) pecan pieces**

½ **teaspoon salt**

Combine all the ingredients in the bowl of a food processor and pulse until the butter or coconut oil pieces are no larger than a pea.

Alternatively, to mix by hand, combine cornmeal, flour, brown sugar, and salt in a medium bowl. Add the butter or coconut oil pieces and toss to coat them in the dry ingredients. Use your fingers to squeeze the butter or coconut oil pieces into pea-size pieces. Sprinkle the vanilla extract over the dry ingredients and butter, then add the pecan pieces and toss once more with your fingers to combine.

Pour the fruit filling into the bottom crust. Using a spatula, smooth the surface of the filling, ensuring the filling reaches the edges evenly.

Sprinkle the crumb over the filling one large spoonful at a time, starting at the outer edge and working your way toward the center. Use your fingers to gently distribute the topping so the thickness is more or less consistent across the center of the pie and slightly thicker near the edges. Do not compress it into the filling.

The crumb can be kept in an airtight container in the freezer for up to 1 year.

NUT CRUMB VARIATION

Substitute the pecan pieces with any nut(s) of your choice: Walnuts, pistachios, and macadamias are all delicious options. Chop them into small pieces before using.

BROWN BUTTER
HAZELNUT-ALMOND STREUSEL

The first pie I tried this with was Black Currant (page 82). I created this recipe to counterbalance the sharp acidity of the filling. I find that it works well with Rhubarb Pie (page 66) for the same reason—the warm, rounded flavors are a complement to the rhubarb's acidity.

½ cup (1 stick/115 g) unsalted butter

⅓ cup (45 g) almonds

⅓ cup (45 g) hazelnuts

¾ cup (95 g) all-purpose flour or gluten-free oat flour, from the freezer

½ cup (100 g) sugar

½ teaspoon salt

1 teaspoon vanilla

In a lightly colored medium saucepan (so that you can see the color of the butter as it cooks—white enamel or stainless steel both work well), melt the butter over medium heat. After the butter melts and begins to bubble, heat for 5 to 10 minutes more, stirring with a wooden spoon, until the butter browns. When the butter is sufficiently browned, small chunks of toasty brown caramelized milk solids will have formed, and the rest of the butter will have a deep, golden-brown hue. Set it aside and allow to cool completely.

In a food processor, pulse the almonds and hazelnuts until they form a rough meal.

In a bowl, combine the nut meal, flour, sugar, and salt and stir well with a fork. Sprinkle the vanilla over the nut meal mixture, stirring to disperse the vanilla as well as possible. Pour the cooled browned butter over the nut meal mixture. Toss lightly with a fork, but don't attempt to mix it completely. Chill completely before using.

Pour the fruit filling into the bottom crust. Using a spatula, smooth the surface of the filling, ensuring the filling reaches the edges evenly.

Sprinkle the streusel over the filling one large spoonful at a time, starting at the outer edge and working your way toward the center. Use your fingers to gently distribute the topping so the thickness is more or less consistent across the center of the pie and slightly thicker near the edges. Do not compress it into the filling.

The streusel can be kept in an airtight container in the freezer for up to 1 year.

SPICED STREUSEL VARIATION

Mix ¼ teaspoon ground cinnamon and ¼ teaspoon cardamom into the sugar before combining with the nut meal, flour, and salt. This variation is delicious on peach, apple, or pear filling.

TWO METHODS OF PAR-BAKING AND BLIND-BAKING SHELLS

To make a pie with a precooked filling, such as a lemon meringue or banana cream pie, you need to "blind-bake" the bottom crust in advance. Blind-baking is simply precooking a crust.

For pies that have a short cooking time, or for custard pies in which the filling cooks faster than the crust, "par-baking" is the way to go. Par-baking is partially baking a crust before the filling is added, so it can bake completely without overcooking the filling.

1. PIE WEIGHT METHOD

Either keep a simple edge or crimp the crust as detailed in the crimped bottom shell tutorial on page 52.

Preheat the oven to 375°F (190°C).

Line the pie shell with a circle of parchment paper. Add dry beans, uncooked rice, or pie weights to reach about two-thirds of the way up the sides of the crust.

To par-bake: Bake the shell for 20 minutes. Let cool, then carefully remove the pie weights and parchment paper.

To blind-bake: Bake the shell for 20 minutes, then carefully remove the pie weights and parchment paper. If you made a crimped edge, gently cover it with a strip of aluminum foil or a pie crust protector. Put the shell back in the oven and bake for 15 minutes more to fully bake the bottom of the crust.

2. PAN SANDWICH METHOD

Recyclable aluminum tins can be very handy for blind-baking and are required for this method, as other types of pans would be too heavy. This method works for simple, uncrimped shells. If you want the elegance of a crimped crust, use the pie weight method.

After transferring your dough sheet into the pie pan, trim the bottom crust by running a knife around the edge. Sprinkle flour over the shell and place another tin snugly inside it, sandwiching the dough sheet between two tins. For best results, place the unbaked shell in the freezer and allow it to reach a hard freeze before baking. This will help prevent shrinkage.

Preheat the oven to 375°F (190°C).

To par-bake: Weigh down the top tin with metal measuring cups or utensils. Bake the shell for 20 minutes. When the crust has cooled completely, remove the upper tin.

To blind-bake: Weigh down the top tin with metal measuring cups or utensils. Bake the shell for 20 minutes, then gently remove the upper tin. Put the shell back in the oven and bake for 15 minutes more.

HOW TO FREEZE A PIE CRUST AND HOW TO STORE A BAKED PIE

Unbaked pie crust freezes very well, and butter crust becomes even flakier after a deep freeze. I recommend freezing dough in the form you're most likely to use it. For custard, nut, chess, or fruit crumb pies, freeze the dough as a crimped shell. For fruit double-crust pies, go ahead and lay each layer of crust in a pie pan (just as you would for a bottom crust). After the crust is removed from the freezer and comes up to room temperature, one of the shells can be filled with fruit fillings, while the other can be gently removed from the other tin and laid over the filling to make a top crust.

To freeze, simply place the prepared shell(s) in their pans in a large sealable freezer bag and press out as much air as possible before completely sealing it shut. Store in the freezer for up to a year and allow the dough to come to room temperature before adding filling and baking.

I do not recommend freezing pies once they are baked. Storage information is included in each recipe, explaining my recommended way of storing each pie throughout the book.

In general, pies that are not meant to be served cold will taste best when stored at room temperature and eaten within a day or two. If you need to keep a custard pie longer than a couple days, however, it's important to keep it in the fridge.

You can extend the shelf life of any fruit, nut, or chess pie by refrigerating it, although it will change the texture of the crust and make the filling more firm.

CHOCOLATE GANACHE FOR BLACK-BOTTOM PIES

Makes enough ganache for one 9-inch (23-cm) black-bottom pie

¼ cup plus 2 tablespoons (90 ml) heavy cream

3¼ ounces (90 g) dark chocolate, chopped into small pieces

¼ teaspoon vanilla

Pinch of salt

1 bottom crust, crimped (½ recipe any crust type; see pages 50 and 52) or 1 bottom crust, crimped and blind-baked (½ recipe any crust type; see pages 50, 52, and 60), depending on your eventual filling choice

"BLACK BOTTOM" IS A RELATIVELY LOOSE TERM USED TO DESCRIBE desserts that have a base layer of chocolate in some form or another. My black-bottom pies are made either by adding a thin layer of chocolate ganache to coat the bottom of a crust before it is baked, as in the black-bottom Almond Chess Pie (page 180), or added to a blind-baked crust for use in a chilled pie, such as the Pistachio Cloud Pie (page 138).

In a small saucepan, heat the cream just until it bubbles. Take the pan off the heat and add the chocolate, whisking until smooth. Add the vanilla and salt and whisk until the ganache is completely smooth. Pour into the bottom crust while still warm. If the ganache feels slightly thick or has cooled a bit, you can still use it—just use a spoon or spatula to spread it around evenly. Place the pie shell in the fridge and allow the chocolate to chill completely, about 45 minutes, before adding filling and baking.

SUGAR SCRAPS

½ cup (100 g) sugar

1 tablespoon ground cinnamon

2 teaspoons ground cardamom

½ teaspoon ground nutmeg

½ teaspoon ground allspice

¼ teaspoon salt

Leftover pastry dough (any type)

Egg Wash (page 56) or maple syrup for a vegan crust

MY PARENTS BAKE PIECES OF THEIR PIE CRUST WITH CINNAMON and sugar, bag them, and sell the "sugar scraps"—in fact, they sell a lot of them, as they are really popular. I prefer to use not only cinnamon but a mix of spices. Snacking on these may just take your mind off a pie that is cooling too slowly.

Preheat the oven to 375°F (190°C).

In a bowl, combine the sugar, spices, and salt.

Using the same method as for how to roll a dough sheet (see page 50), roll the leftover pie crust to ⅛ inch (3 mm) thick and brush it with egg wash or maple syrup. Sprinkle with the spiced sugar, as lightly or heavily as you'd like. (Depending on how much pastry dough you have, you may end up with a lot of leftover spiced sugar. You can store it indefinitely in an airtight container at room temperature.) Cut the pie crust into whatever shapes you'd like with a knife or a cookie cutter. Transfer the crust pieces to a baking sheet lined with parchment paper.

Bake for 25 to 30 minutes, or until the pastry pieces are puffed, crisp, and no longer doughy. Transfer to a cooling rack. Enjoy as soon as they've cooled, or keep them in an airtight container at room temperature for up to a week.

BAKED
FRUIT PIES

We live in an age when we have access to a wider variety of foods than ever before. You're in New York but you want peaches in December? No problem, they're shipped in from Chile. You want strawberries on Valentine's Day? There are stacks of plastic clamshells full of massive strawberries from Southern California right there in your local grocery store.

While the hyperavailability of produce year-round can be convenient, I don't think it always adds to our quality of life. When we get used to the tastes and textures of subpar berries shipped across the country, we sometimes forget just how earth-shattering a juicy, truly ripe strawberry can be in its season. We blunt the pleasure of anticipation and get out of sync with the seasons.

One powerful way we can reconnect to the joy of food is by making pies with seasonal produce. When you make the recipes in this section, I challenge you to seek out the most gloriously ripe, vibrantly flavorful produce you can find. Rhubarb should be fresh and crisp, strawberries should be deep-red and fragrant, and stone fruit should be achingly ripe—no matter if it's bruised. This usually means getting acquainted with your local farmers' market, or perhaps visiting a farm and picking it yourself, or even foraging in a park.

Because we are relying on flavorful fruit for our pies, these recipes do not call for a lot of sugar. They start with 1¼ to 1½ pounds (570 to 680 g) of fruit, so all the fillings end up in the same weight range, which means they can bake at a rate that allows the filling and crust to finish cooking at the same time. Moreover, this filling weight makes a pie with an ideal filling-to-crust ratio. Sure, pies with apples stacked half a foot high look cartoonishly cute, but the recipes in this section will give you balance, bite after bite.

I recommend tapioca starch as a thickener for the fruit pies because it has a neutral taste and sets up with fruit juice as a transparent gel. Technically cornstarch has the same thickening power, so it can be substituted 1:1, but it tends to make a cloudier filling. While many old-fashioned recipes use flour as a thickener, I find that it adds an off-putting texture to pie fillings and dulls the flavors of the fruit.

Any of these pies can be made gluten-free by using a gluten-free crust and topping. Aside from Autumn Pear Pie (page 92), Maple Butter Apple Pie (page 100), and Mince Pie (page 105), all these recipes can be vegan if prepared with a vegan crust and brushed with maple syrup instead of egg wash (see page 56).

RHUBARB PIE

Makes one 9-inch (23-cm) pie

1¼ pounds (565 g) rhubarb, cut into ½-inch (12-mm) pieces

1 teaspoon lemon juice

¾ cup (150 g) sugar

2 tablespoons plus 2 teaspoons tapioca starch

¼ teaspoon salt

1 bottom crust, crimped (½ recipe any crust type; see pages 50 and 52)

1 recipe Brown Butter Hazelnut-Almond Streusel (page 59)

RHUBARB IS NOT A FRUIT—IT'S A VEGETABLE WITH POISONOUS leaves and a thick, acidic stalk—but it tends to be treated like one nonetheless. While it fulfills various functions in other cuisines, appearing in jams, compotes, and even in a traditional Afghan stew with lamb, it's mostly known for pie in the United States, where it has the nickname "pie plant." A pie made with only rhubarb might not be as glamorous and broadly appealing as its rosy-hued cousin, Strawberry Rhubarb (page 68), but it sure is tart and tasty—and it's also the first fresh "fruit" pie we can make in the spring! Look for rhubarb that is firm in texture and bright in color. As with most fruits and vegetables, there are many varieties of rhubarb out there. If you prefer a pink-hued pie, choose stalks that are deep red toward the bottom, but just know that the humble green stalks are tasty too! To contrast the acidic flavor and soft, stewed texture of the rhubarb filling, I bake this pie with a crunchy, toasty hazelnut-almond streusel, but you can make it as a double-crust pie if you prefer pure, untempered rhubarb flavor. Try either version with a couple spoonfuls of Custard Sauce (page 227).

Preheat the oven to 400°F (205°C).

In a large bowl, combine the rhubarb and lemon juice. In a small bowl, whisk together the sugar, tapioca starch, and salt, making sure that the starch is evenly dispersed. Pour the sugar mixture over the rhubarb and stir to coat. Pour the filling into the bottom crust, making sure to scrape the entire contents from the sides of the bowl into the pie.

Top the filling with the streusel according to the instructions on page 59. Place the pie on a baking sheet to collect any juices that bubble over and bake for 20 minutes, then reduce the heat to 375°F (190°C) and continue to bake for 40 minutes more, or until the filling has been bubbling for at least 10 minutes.

Transfer the pie to a cooling rack and allow to cool for at least 45 minutes before serving. Serve warm or at room temperature. The pie will keep for up to 3 days at room temperature.

STRAWBERRY-RHUBARB PIE

Makes one 9-inch (23-cm) pie

1¼ cups (190 g) hulled strawberries (If you are using very petite strawberries, leave them whole. For larger strawberries, cut them in half.)

3½ cups (375 g) rhubarb cut into ½-inch (12-mm) pieces

1 teaspoon lemon juice

⅔ cup (135 g) sugar

3 tablespoons tapioca starch

¼ teaspoon salt

1 recipe any crust type, bottom crust prepared to make a double-crust pie (see pages 50 and 53)

Egg Wash (page 56)

AT THE RISK OF REVEALING MYSELF TO BE A PIE SNOB (SURPRISE!), I must admit that I'm rarely impressed with strawberry-rhubarb pie when I order it at a bakery or restaurant. If it isn't made with super flavorful strawberries and the proper ratio of rhubarb to berries, the magic just isn't there, and it tastes like a bland, sour strawberry pie. You might think that a 2:1 ratio of rhubarb to strawberries would be overpowering, but it's actually precisely what's needed to concoct a flavor that is so much more than the sum of its parts, almost like some tropical fruit you're discovering for the first time. My favorite way to make this pie is in a simple double crust, which lets the filling sing.

Preheat the oven to 400°F (205°C).

In a large bowl, combine the berries and rhubarb with the lemon juice. In a small bowl, whisk together the sugar, tapioca starch, and salt, making sure that the starch is evenly dispersed. Pour the sugar mixture over the fruit and stir gently to coat. Pour the filling into the bottom crust, making sure to scrape the entire contents from the sides of the bowl into the pie.

Top the pie with the top crust according to the instructions on page 53. Brush the top crust with the egg wash. Place the pie on a baking sheet to collect any juices that bubble over and bake for 20 minutes, then reduce the heat to 375°F (190°C) and continue to bake for 40 minutes more, or until the filling has been bubbling for at least 10 minutes.

Transfer the pie to a cooling rack and allow to cool for at least 1 hour before serving. Serve warm or at room temperature. The pie will keep for up to 3 days at room temperature.

JUNEBERRY PIE

Makes one 9-inch (23-cm) pie

1½ pounds (680 g) juneberries

2 tablespoons lemon juice

⅓ cup (65 g) sugar

2 tablespoons tapioca starch

¼ teaspoon salt

1 recipe any crust type, bottom crust prepared to make a double-crust pie (see pages 50 and 54)

Egg Wash (page 56)

JUNEBERRY TREES CAN BE FOUND IN THE WILD OVER HUGE swaths of the northern United States and Canada, where they're often used for landscaping in urban development and office parking lots. In some regions, farmers are experimenting with growing them commercially, but you probably won't find juneberries at the farmers' market any time soon, much less the grocery store. If you get your hands on some from a reputable source, I encourage you to make them into a pie. The dark berries, also called serviceberries or saskatoons, resemble blueberries and taste like a cross between a blueberry and a pear, with a lovely almond flavor that becomes more pronounced after baking. While they're plenty sweet, they don't have much natural acidity, so lots of lemon juice is in order. I recommend making this as a double-crust pie so that the unique flavor of the juneberries can really come through.

Preheat the oven to 400°F (205°C).

In a large bowl, combine the juneberries with the lemon juice. In a small bowl, whisk together the sugar, tapioca starch, and salt, making sure that the starch is evenly dispersed. Pour the sugar mixture over the berries and gently stir to coat—juneberries are very delicate. Pour the filling into the bottom crust, making sure to scrape the entire contents from the sides of the bowl into the pie.

Top the pie with lattice crust according to the instructions on page 54. Brush the top crust with the egg wash. Place the pie on a baking sheet to collect any juices that bubble over and bake for 20 minutes, then reduce the heat to 375°F (190°C) and continue to bake for 40 minutes more, or until the filling has been bubbling for at least 10 minutes.

Transfer the pie to a cooling rack and allow to cool for at least 30 minutes before serving. Serve warm or at room temperature. The pie will keep for up to 3 days at room temperature.

SUMMER PEACH (OR NECTARINE) PIE

Makes one 9-inch (23-cm) pie

1½ pounds (680 g) peach slices
  (skins removed) or nectarine slices
  (skin on), plus their juices (see Note)

1 tablespoon lemon juice

½ cup (100 g) sugar

2 tablespoons plus 1 teaspoon tapioca
  starch

¼ teaspoon salt

1 recipe any crust type, bottom crust
  prepared to make a double-crust pie
  (see pages 50 and 54)

Egg Wash (page 56)

Note: Depending on the water content,
size of the pit, and other variables, it
may take just a few or several pieces
of whole fruit to make the called-
for weight of slices. To be safe, buy
2 pounds (910 g) of fruit. As you slice
the fruit, take care to collect the juices
in a large bowl so that you don't miss
any of the flavor, and include the
juice in the total weight. (Weigh the
empty bowl first so you don't count its
weight in the total.)

THIS IS THE PIE TO MAKE WHEN SUMMER'S PEACHES AND
nectarines are at their sweetest. But here's the thing about peaches
and nectarines: They're really, really similar. Both can have white
or yellow flesh, and both can come in clingstone varieties (in which
the flesh sticks to the pit) or freestone varieties (in which the pit and
flesh separate easily). In fact, they are almost genetically identical,
the main difference being that nectarines possess a recessive gene
for smooth, thin skin, while peaches have a fuzzy, thicker skin.

With all their similarities, it might seem silly to pick a side, but
you'll still find me on team nectarine. Why? Stone fruit skin holds
so much of its flavor, and you can use nectarines with their skins
on, whereas many people find peach skin to be off-putting in a pie.
At the bakery, we go through the trouble of blanching and peeling
fresh New Jersey peaches, but if you want to make a "peach" pie with
nectarines, your secret is safe with me. I recommend making this as
a lattice crust pie since it's so juicy.

Preheat the oven to 400°F (205°C).

In a large bowl, combine the peach or nectarine slices with the lemon
juice. In a small bowl, whisk together the sugar, tapioca starch, and
salt, making sure that the starch is evenly dispersed. Pour the sugar
mixture over the slices and gently stir to coat. Pour the filling into the
bottom crust, making sure to scrape the entire contents from the sides
of the bowl into the pie.

Top the pie with a lattice crust according to the instructions on page 54.
Brush the top crust with the egg wash. Place the pie on a baking sheet to
collect any juices that bubble over and bake for 20 minutes, then reduce the
heat to 375°F (190°C) and continue to bake for 40 minutes more, or until the
filling has been bubbling for at least 10 minutes.

Transfer the pie to a cooling rack and allow to cool for at least 1 hour
before serving. Serve warm or at room temperature. The pie will keep
for up to 3 days at room temperature.

AUTUMN PEACH (OR NECTARINE) PIE

Makes one 9-inch (23-cm) pie

1½ pounds (680 g) peach slices (skins removed) or nectarine slices (skin on), plus their juices (see Note on page 72)

1 teaspoon lemon juice

Scrapings from ¼ vanilla bean, or ¼ teaspoon vanilla extract

½ cup (100 g) sugar

2 tablespoons plus 1 teaspoon tapioca starch

¼ teaspoon salt

⅛ teaspoon ground cinnamon

⅛ teaspoon ground cardamom

⅛ teaspoon ground nutmeg

1 bottom crust of Butter Pastry Dough (page 38), crimped (½ recipe; see pages 50 and 52)

1 recipe Cornmeal-Pecan Crumb (page 58)

IN NEW YORK, PEACH AND NECTARINE SEASON EXTENDS INTO September, at which point I get cravings for warm, spiced flavors. A little less lemon, a touch of vanilla, and a subtle blend of spices is all it takes to carry peaches over the threshold into autumn. I recommend considering a bottom butter crust and a cornmeal-pecan crumb on top, which gives this pie a pleasant crunch and even more autumnal flavor.

Preheat the oven to 400°F (205°C).

In a large bowl, combine the peach or nectarine slices, lemon juice, and vanilla. In a small bowl, whisk together the sugar, tapioca starch, salt, cinnamon, cardamom, and nutmeg, making sure that the starch is evenly dispersed. Pour the sugar mixture over the slices and gently stir to combine. Pour the filling into the bottom crust, making sure to scrape the entire contents from the sides of the bowl into the pie.

Top the filling with the crumb according to the instructions on page 58. Place the pie on a baking sheet to collect any juices that bubble over and bake for 20 minutes, then reduce the heat to 375°F (190°C) and continue to bake for 40 minutes more, or until the filling has been bubbling for at least 10 minutes.

Transfer the pie to a cooling rack and allow to cool for at least 45 minutes before serving. Serve warm or at room temperature. The pie will keep for up to 3 days at room temperature.

SOUR CHERRY PIE

Makes one 9-inch (23-cm) pie

1½ pounds (680 g) pitted sour cherries, fresh or frozen (see Note)

½ teaspoon lemon juice

⅛ teaspoon almond extract (optional)

¾ cup (150 g) sugar

⅓ cup (45 g) tapioca starch

⅛ teaspoon salt

1 recipe any crust type, bottom crust prepared to make a double-crust pie (see pages 50 and 54)

Egg Wash (page 56)

Note: If you are pitting fresh sour cherries, buy about 2 pounds (910 g) to ensure you end up with enough fruit for the pie. As you pit the fruit, take care to collect the juices in a large bowl so that you don't miss any of the flavor, and include the juice in the total weight. To take full advantage of sour cherry season, invest in a cherry pitter (see bottom image on page 24). This handly little tool positions the fruit so that the pit can be popped right out, and some can even pit multiple cherries at once.

IF YOU'VE EVER EATEN A CHERRY PIE, ODDS ARE IT WAS MADE WITH sour cherries—after all, they're also known as "pie cherries." Michigan in particular is known for its delicious sour cherries. But when I opened up shop in New York City, I was pleased to discover that New York State is among the top five producers of sour cherries in the United States. Their season lasts for only a couple of fleeting summer weeks, which is why more than 90 percent of the sour cherry crop in the country is sold frozen. That said, it's still not easy to find frozen sour cherries at the store, so if you find yourself wanting delicious sour cherry pie for more than two weeks of the year, your best bet is to buy tons of them fresh, pit them yourself, and freeze them to use whenever you get the craving (see page 28 for tips on freezing fresh fruit). Lattice crust cherry pie is aesthetic perfection, and also practical because of the super-juicy filling. Consider serving your cherry pie with a scoop of vanilla ice cream—a creamy contrast for the tart cherries—on top.

Preheat the oven to 400°F (205°C).

In a large bowl, combine the cherries, lemon juice, and almond extract, if using. In a small bowl, whisk together the sugar, tapioca starch, and salt, making sure that the starch is evenly dispersed. Pour the sugar mixture over the cherries and gently stir to coat. If you're using frozen fruit, allow the mixture to sit for 30 minutes before assembling the pie, and stir before pouring it into the crust. Pour the filling into the bottom crust, making sure to scrape the entire contents from the sides of the bowl into the pie.

Top the pie with a lattice crust according to the instructions on page 54. Brush the top crust with the egg wash. Place the pie on a baking sheet to collect any juices that bubble over. Bake for 20 minutes, then reduce the heat to 375°F (190°C) and continue to bake for 40 minutes more, or until the filling has been bubbling for at least 10 minutes.

Transfer the pie to a cooling rack and allow to cool for at least 1 hour before serving. Serve warm or at room temperature. The pie will keep for up to 3 days at room temperature.

GREG QUINN, CURRANT CRUSADER

Meet Greg Quinn, currant farmer and owner of CurrantC, a company offering all manner of currant products. Like most farmers I know, Greg is intensely devoted, knowledgeable, and passionate about the produce he grows. Unlike most farmers I know, he has a TED Talk and single-handedly worked to overturn a state law in order to grow the fruit he loves so much.

For the past century, black currants have been a consistent presence in European cuisine, but they are very rare in the United States. In Europe, they are celebrated for their exceptionally tart flavor; beautiful, deep purple juice; and considerable health benefits. The anthocyanins that give the berries their gorgeous color also make them an excellent source of antioxidants. Black currants have four times as much vitamin C as oranges and twice the potassium of a

banana. So why has it taken us so long to appreciate them?

In 1911, the cultivation of black currants was banned in order to protect the lumber industry, because of the plants' alleged tendency to harbor a fungus that was detrimental to white pines. After Greg Quinn bought Walnut Grove Farm in Staatsburg, New York, in 1999 and was researching crops to grow, he came across some information about the black currant ban. Having run a restaurant for servicemen in Bavaria for several years, he was familiar with the fruit and quite enjoyed it—it hadn't occurred to him that its lack of popularity in the United States was due to a legal issue. While he isn't a plant scientist, he did spend more than twenty years growing plants and educating visitors at the New York Botanical Garden, so he knows a thing or two about

In addition to growing currants, Greg tends to animals and keeps bees for his "Currant Farm Honey."

Note: Perhaps you're thinking to yourself, "Currants . . . I see dried currants all the time at the grocery store!" However, the dried fruits labeled "Zante currants" are not currants at all but actually a type of small seedless raisin of the Black Corinth grape variety. They were imported from the Greek island of Corinth into English markets under the name "Raisins de Corinth," and some say that the name Zante currants stemmed from this (the second syllable of "raisin," pronounced in its original French, sounds somewhat like "zan"). Others say that Corinth was mistranslated as currant, and that the raisins that later came from the island of Zakynthos were labeled "Zakynthos currants," and Zakynthos was translated to "Zante." Based on phonetics alone, I find the former explanation easier to swallow. Regardless of how they got their names, it's important to know that Zante currants are not dried currants but dried Black Corinth grapes. For the dried black currants called for in the Mince and Savory Mincemeat Pies (pages 105 and 206), Zante currants won't fit the bill.

growing plants. It appeared to him that the science underpinning the ban (which had converted from a federal ban to a state-level ban in the 1960s) was shaky at best. He set out to investigate and discovered that many varieties of black currant bushes were resistant to the fungus in question, so there was no reason that cultivation of black currants had to be detrimental to white pines. The bigger challenge was getting state lawmakers to care enough to overturn a decades-old law that affected, well, just about no one.

But Greg is not one to shy away from a challenge. He started visiting the state legislature in Albany regularly. Some lawmakers were very frank with him: It simply wasn't an issue that voters were concerned with, so it wasn't worth their time. In response, he took to plying their law clerks and secretaries with baked goods in hopes that they'd squeeze him into a vacant meeting slot. Eventually a reporter at the *Wall Street Journal* caught wind of his efforts, and the ensuing article landed the cover. Unfortunately Greg didn't like it at all—it took the side of the lumber industry and seemed to miss the point about the demonstrable harmlessness of black currant cultivation. On top of that, the journalist posited that black currants were simply too tart for the American palate! However, in this case, any publicity was good publicity, and the headline lobbyist's battle to develop New York's forbidden fruit caught the attention of a lawmaker who also served on an agricultural committee and thought there was plenty of potential in legalizing black currants, and things got rolling from there. In 2004, the governor signed a law overturning the ban, and a letter from the governor now hangs proudly in Greg's office.

Greg now has the largest currant farm in the United States and holds the patents for all the black currant varieties imported from Poland, where they are grown extensively. He's in the interesting position of building demand for a fruit that many people just aren't familiar with, while also building his business. When I first bought Greg's black currants from a farm-to-restaurant distributor in 2016, I had never baked with them before and was merely curious. I developed a black currant pie recipe that I enjoyed very much, but I was worried that its intense tartness would overwhelm our customers' palates. Granted, we offer fair warning about it when describing the pie, but I was pleasantly surprised to see just how much of our customer base enjoys the intensity just as much as I do! I feel like I'm making up for lost time with this beloved fruit and try to work it into any recipe it might fit. We now use black currants in our mince pies, in linzer cookies in place of raspberry jam, and to make our own crème de cassis, to which we add sparkling wine for Kir Royale cocktails at our café. It turns out that this formerly forbidden fruit can be quite at home stateside, as well.

BLACK CURRANT PIE

Makes one 9-inch (23-cm) pie

1¼ pounds (570 g) black currants, fresh or frozen

¾ cup (150 g) sugar

2 tablespoons plus 2 teaspoons tapioca starch

Pinch of salt

1 bottom crust, crimped (½ recipe any crust type; see pages 50 and 52)

1 recipe crumb or streusel topping (see pages 57–59)

BLACK CURRANTS ARE IN SEASON FOR JUST A FEW PRECIOUS weeks in the summer, and while I try to make at least one pie then, I love to bake with frozen currants in the dead of winter. Their deep and intense flavor, vibrant acidity, and, of course, extraordinary vitamin C content make this pie a shot of summer sunshine right when you need it the most. If you'd like to temper the intense tartness, I recommend making this pie with the Brown Butter Hazelnut-Almond Streusel topping (page 59), which balances out the flavors nicely, or serving à la mode.

Preheat the oven to 400°F (205°C).

Place the currants in a large bowl. In a small bowl, whisk together the sugar, tapioca starch, and salt, making sure that the starch is evenly dispersed. Pour the sugar mixture over the currants and toss to coat, being especially gentle if using fresh fruit. If using frozen fruit, allow the mixture to sit for 30 minutes before assembling the pie, and stir the fruit mixture before pouring it into the crust. Pour the filling into the bottom crust, making sure to scrape the entire contents from the sides of the bowl into the pie.

Top the filling with the crumb or streusel according to the instructions on pages 58–59. Place the pie on a baking sheet to collect any juices that bubble over. Bake for 20 minutes, then reduce the heat to 375°F (190°C) and continue to bake for 40 minutes more, or until the filling has been bubbling for at least 10 minutes.

Transfer the pie to a cooling rack and allow to cool for at least 1 hour before serving. Serve warm or at room temperature. The pie will keep for up to 3 days at room temperature.

NATIVE BLUEBERRIES

I've always exclusively used wild blueberries in my pies because of their amazingly concentrated flavor. I knew that one day—since I like to know where my ingredients come from—I'd be compelled to visit their place of origin. One August I did just that, visiting Ruth Fiske and Nicolas Lindholm at their farm in the Blue Hill Peninsula on the coast of Maine. (I initially discovered this small farm when searching for independent wild blueberry wholesalers. Because of the small scale of their business, they cannot wholesale, but they were happy to have me visit!)

Ruth and Nicolas bought some land in 1996 and set about growing various vegetables and wild blueberries to sell locally. Now they have a nice big vegetable garden for themselves, and for their livelihood they tend to more than one hundred acres of wild blueberry fields—some on their own land, others leased.

When I arrived at their farm and homestead on the first evening, I expected to see fields of blueberries—but I didn't. On a brief tour of the farm, I saw the home that Ruth and Nicolas built for themselves, a tiny shed-size house their son was inhabiting for the summer, and their barn and sorting facility. I sat on their porch and observed some sheep rooting around while Nicolas took a break from the evening's work to tell me about his family's history and how he manages the land and his staff. The only blueberries I saw were in a walk-in cooler in the barn. I thought the berry fields must be on another part of the property.

The next morning I tagged along with Nicolas and his crew—a group of young vagabonds who live out of a van—to a field that he'd been managing for a friend. When I arrived, I saw the crew scooping their rakes on the ground. It was only then I realized that the

Nicolas Lindholm raking wild blueberries by the forest's edge

night before I had been surrounded by wild blueberries and just hadn't noticed. Wild blueberry plants are small and inconspicuous, many of them rising only a few inches off the ground. All I had to do was look down, but instead I had been looking for neat rows of short berry bushes, something that resembled the kind of farming I was familiar with. *After all, they're called wild blueberries, and how wild could they be if they were farmed?*

The truth, Nicolas says, is that "wild" might not be the best descriptor for a plant that is managed so intensively by humans—"native" is the better word. These blueberries have grown in the forests of New England and the Canadian maritime provinces for more than ten thousand years. They can even survive without their seeds being distributed by humans or animals, as they self-propagate under the soil by shooting out rhizomes.

Ruth and Nicolas grow their berries organically, which many people erroneously assume is always the case when it comes to

wild blueberries. Not so: Conventional wild blueberry farmers can use synthetic fertilizers, pesticides, herbicides, and fungicides—an arguably shortsighted approach with the intent to obliterate resource competition and increase yield. This ravages the soil, diminishes biodiversity, and makes farmers increasingly dependent on the use of synthetic fertilizers.

While Ruth and Nicolas are indeed growing only one crop exclusively, none of the usual concerns about monocrop agriculture apply here. When they're managed organically, wild blueberry fields are rich in diversity. Interspersed with the blueberries are tons of other life-forms. Of the many you can see with the naked eye are insects and arachnids, moss and fungi, plants and grasses, and even other berries. The blueberries themselves also display a wide genetic range. Some are purple and shiny, with barely any bloom (the powdery-looking coating found on a blueberry's skin, which is actually a natural wax), while some are light dusty blue. Some are miniscule (these you'll only encounter if you pick them yourself) and very occasionally, you might find one approaching the size of a conventional blueberry.

Since wild blueberries don't need us to propagate them, wild blueberry farmers don't do many of the things that other farmers do, like select seeds, plant rows, or till soil. Instead, they keep the forest at bay, giving the scrubby bushes sun exposure to help them produce more tasty fruit. After all, these plants have been dwelling on the forest floor of this region for millennia, but if it weren't for farmers like Ruth and Nicolas, the forest would simply overtake the clearings once again, reducing the amount of fruit produced. The other major intervention they undertake is quite dramatic: a biennial field burning. On alternating fields each winter, they spread straw and ignite it, setting in motion a controlled burn that reduces the bushes to ash. One might think that a farmer would be devastated to see their field in flames, but this destruction spurs the rhizomes under the surface to give rise to young, vibrant shoots with higher yields of berries.

Unlike most wild blueberry farmers, who sell more than 95 percent of their crop frozen through large distributors, Nicolas and Ruth have managed to sell most of their berries locally in season—late July into September. Part of what enables them to do this is offering a meticulously sorted, high-quality product at farmers' markets and selling large orders to self-organizing groups of customers. They use a winnowing machine that sorts out tiny berries, clusters, and stems, then have three to four people working a conveyor belt to remove any mushy berries. The end result is containers of perfectly intact berries—*only* berries. No extra work or washing for the customers, since they're organic and painstakingly sorted already.

As for the 5 to 10 percent of the wild blueberries that they do freeze, you'd be hard-pressed to match their quality. When you open a box, you might mistake them for fresh berries if not for the vapor that rises from them. Unlike the frozen wild blueberries at the grocery store (which are still good for baking, don't get me wrong), their bloom is intact and none of their juices haven't bled out. We don't need them to be this perfect, but they are.

Nicolas and Ruth could certainly get away with not offering such unparalleled quality—with not being so principled and responsible. They could do things the easier way: increase yield with chemical fertilizer, use pesticides to get rid of competition, harvest with machines, be a little less meticulous, sell to bigger food companies. They could ask their laborers to work twelve hours a day for meager pay, rather than offering fair compensation and a forty-hour work week with weekends off (an extreme rarity in my experience!). But this is the life they've chosen, the land they've vowed to care for, and the plant that they've partnered with, and they fulfill their roles with stalwart compassion and care.

WILD BLUEBERRY PIE

Makes one 9-inch (23-cm) pie

1½ pounds (680 g) wild blueberries, fresh or frozen

⅓ cup (65 g) sugar

2 tablespoons tapioca starch

⅛ teaspoon salt

1 tablespoon lemon juice

1 recipe any crust type, bottom crust prepared to make a double-crust pie (see pages 50 and 54), or 1 bottom crust, crimped (½ recipe any crust type; see pages 50 and 52) and 1 recipe crumb topping (see page 57)

Egg Wash (page 56), if using a top crust

WILD BLUEBERRIES ARE TREMENDOUSLY FLAVORFUL THANKS TO their antioxidant-rich skin. My recipe uses a modest amount of sugar to let the berries shine and plenty of lemon juice for brightness. Since wild blueberries have more skin and less flesh than their conventional cousins, they require less starch to thicken. That said, if you cut this pie while it's hot, expect a deluge of beautiful purple juice!

This filling is a nice option for a lattice pie, because of the juiciness and beautiful color. If you make a gluten-free or vegan version, try topping it with a Cornmeal-Pecan Crumb (page 58), which provides a lovely textural contrast. Note that I do not recommend making this recipe with conventional blueberries, as the other ingredients would need to be adjusted and wild blueberries are far superior in pies.

Preheat the oven to 400°F (205°C).

Place the berries in a large bowl. In a small bowl, whisk together the sugar, tapioca starch, and salt, making sure that the starch is evenly dispersed. Pour the sugar mixture over the berries and toss to coat. Pour the lemon juice over the mixture and stir gently. If using frozen fruit, allow the mixture to sit for 30 minutes before assembling the pie, and stir the fruit before pouring it into the crust. Pour the filling into the bottom crust, making sure to scrape the entire contents from the sides of the bowl into the pie.

Top the pie with a lattice crust according to the instructions on page 54 or top the filling with the crumb according to the instructions on page 57. Brush the top crust, if using, with the egg wash. Place the pie on a baking sheet to collect any juices that bubble over. Bake for 20 minutes, then reduce the heat to 375°F (190°C) and continue to bake for 40 minutes more, or until the filling has been bubbling for at least 10 minutes.

Transfer the pie to a cooling rack and allow to cool for at least 1 hour before serving. Serve warm or at room temperature. The pie will keep for up to 3 days at room temperature.

MAPLE-WILD BLUEBERRY PIE

Makes one 9-inch (23-cm) pie

3 tablespoons tapioca starch

⅛ teaspoon salt

½ cup (120 ml) maple syrup

1½ pounds (680 g) wild blueberries, fresh or frozen

Zest of half a lemon

1 tablespoon lemon juice

1 recipe Corn Pastry Dough (page 39), bottom crust prepared to make a double-crust pie (see pages 50 and 53)

Egg Wash (page 56)

THIS RECIPE COMBINES THE INDIGENOUS BERRIES OF THE NORTHEAST with the area's inimitable natural sweetener, maple syrup. If you want the maple flavor to come through strongly, use dark maple syrup, which has a more robust, caramelized flavor. Lemon is a natural complement to maple, so lemon zest is included along with lemon juice for some extra zing. You can choose any pastry crust you like, but it's especially fun with a corn crust, considering that, like wild blueberries and maple syrup, corn is indigenous to North America.

Preheat the oven to 400°F (205°C).

In a small bowl, whisk together the tapioca starch and salt. Gradually whisk in the maple syrup, making a slurry.

Place the berries in a large bowl. Pour the maple-starch slurry over them, scraping the bowl to ensure all the slurry is on the berries. Add the lemon zest and juice, then gently stir to coat. If using frozen fruit, allow it to sit for 30 minutes before assembling the pie, and stir the fruit before pouring it into the crust. Pour the filling into the bottom crust, making sure to scrape the entire contents from the sides of the bowl into the pie.

Top the pie with the top crust according to the instructions on page 53. Brush the top crust with the egg wash. Place the pie on a baking sheet to collect any juices that bubble over. Bake for 20 minutes, then reduce the heat to 375°F (190°C) and continue to bake for 40 minutes more, or until the filling has been bubbling for at least 10 minutes.

Transfer the pie to a cooling rack and allow to cool completely before serving to make slicing and serving easier. The pie will keep for up to 3 days at room temperature.

AUTUMN PEAR PIE

Makes one 9-inch (23-cm) pie

3 tablespoons unsalted butter

3 tablespoons maple syrup

⅛ teaspoon ground nutmeg

⅛ teaspoon ground cardamom

Pinch of ground cloves

1½ pounds (680 g) thinly sliced
Asian pears, skins intact

⅓ cup (65 g) sugar

¼ teaspoon salt

2 tablespoons tapioca starch

1 tablespoon lemon juice

½ teaspoon orange zest

½ teaspoon lime zest

1 bottom crust, crimped (½ recipe any
crust type; see pages 50 and 52)

1 recipe Cornmeal-Pecan Crumb,
made with pistachios in place of
pecans (page 58)

THIS PIE IS FULL OF COMPLEX AND CONTRASTING FLAVORS—WARM spices, rich butter, zesty citrus. Asian pears maintain their firm, crunchy texture through baking, so it's best to slice them very thinly. I find the texture to be lovely, especially when the pie is warm. However, if you prefer a more tender filling, substitute half of the Asian pears with soft Bartlett pears. Since the filling contains butter, this pie is not suitable for a vegan preparation. It pairs beautifully with a dollop of Maple Whipped Cream (page 228) and pear brandy.

Preheat the oven to 400°F (205°C).

In a lightly colored, large saucepan (so that you can see the color of the butter as it cooks—white enamel or stainless steel both work well), melt the butter over medium heat. After the butter melts and begins to bubble, heat for 5 to 10 minutes more, stirring with a wooden spoon, until the butter browns. When the butter is sufficiently browned, small chunks of toasty brown caramelized milk solids will have formed, and the rest of the butter will have a deep, golden-brown hue. Remove from the heat and whisk in the maple syrup, nutmeg, cardamom, and cloves. Add the pear slices and stir to coat.

In a small bowl, whisk together the sugar, salt, and tapioca starch, making sure that the starch is evenly dispersed. Pour the sugar mixture over the pears and gently stir to coat. Add the lemon juice and orange and lime zests and gently stir until evenly distributed. Pour the filling into the bottom crust, making sure to scrape the entire contents from the sides of the pan into the pie.

Top the filling with the crumb according to the instructions on page 58. Place the pie on a baking sheet to collect any juices that bubble over. Bake for 20 minutes, then reduce the heat to 375°F (190°C) and continue to bake for 40 minutes more, or until the filling has been bubbling for at least 10 minutes.

Transfer the pie to a cooling rack and allow to cool completely before serving to make slicing and serving easier. The pie will keep for up to 3 days at room temperature.

APPLE PEOPLE

I've met a handful of apple people—enough to know that they're a type.

One of them, the farmer from whom I buy most of my apples, grows seventy-four kinds of apples in his orchard. I could use a different kind of apple every week at my shop, and it would take me nearly a year and a half to go through all his apples.

Another one, whose cider we sell by the glass in our café, came to our first meeting with an album's worth of photos of apples and apple trees. At first he seemed slightly self-conscious when I exclaimed, "Oh, you brought photos!" but when he saw that I was more enthused than amused, he was relieved. What can I say? I'm an apple people person.

Another cider maker popped into my shop one day wearing a backpack, which made him look like a kid on the first day of school.

He "casually" asked about our apple pie, acting like he just happened to be in the neighborhood, but he had a barely concealed giddiness that made me cut to the chase and ask what was in the bag. It was full of apples, of course—he grows 150 varieties of apples upstate, and would I like to try some? Why yes, stranger with a sack full of apples, the answer is yes. There were Northern Spy (also known as Northern Pie; some say there's no better pie apple), a hometown hero named Newtown Pippin (which first grew from seed in Queens in the seventeenth century and later proved to be sufficiently well-adapted to southern climes to be favored by Thomas Jefferson), and some Calville Blanc d'Hiver (a rustic, painterly apple from France that you can see in Claude Monet's *Still Life with Apples and Grapes*). He wanted to know how each kind would fare in a pie. It compelled us to collaborate on some single-varietal apple

Left: Cider maker and apple afficionado Gidon Coll's Hudson Valley Apple Project is an orchard featuring more than 150 apple varietals. Among them are apples that taste like pears or pineapples, European and American heirlooms, an apple from the Caucuses (where apples originated) with shocking blood-red flesh, as well as brand-new varietals being tested by Cornell University.

Opposite: My daughter, Eloisa, was determined to try at least one bite of every apple she could get her hands on at Hudson Valley Apple Project. Remarkably, we made it back home to Brooklyn without any stomachaches.

pies to share with other apple people at a cider festival, just because it's fun to share apple things with apple people.

At that festival there was a little redheaded girl whose parents named Pippin. A pippin is a fine-tasting apple from a tree that was raised from seed (which is a rarity, as I'll explain); all a parent can hope for is that their kid will be a good apple, so why not bestow that optimism in her name? I think that apple people are forever drawn to the tender place where optimism meets fate.

Apples don't grow true to seed. Each apple seed carries with it a distinct set of genes that could possibly result in a delightful pippin but is more likely to result in a bitter crabapple, better suited for cider than a supermarket shelf. In order to cultivate specific varietals of apples, a section of stem from a tree with the desired characteristics, called scion wood, is grafted onto the rootstock of another tree

that is selected for its suitability for the soil and climate of the orchard. Thus the apple trees you see in commercial orchards are all pretty much pieced together like a bunch of Frankenstein's monsters, wholly reliant on humans for their propagation in exchange for offering predictable qualities of taste, texture, appearance, and storability.

All this to say that despite the fact that we tend to see the same handful of varieties in every grocery store, there's virtually limitless potential for diversity when it comes to apples. I think that the dizzying possibilities of apples yet to be discovered, or those hidden in a forgotten orchard, or those lost to history, are what make apple people seem, at times, fanatical.

There's not an apple person I've met who doesn't have some of Johnny Appleseed's zeal. Myths surrounding Johnny Appleseed portray him as a fantastical vagabond in

96

a tin-pot hat with a connection to nature and animals, who was just obsessed with apples. Apocryphal hat aside, he was indeed eccentric. In his travels as a self-appointed missionary of the mystical Swedenborgian Church, he preceded waves of settlers on the frontier and planted countless apple seeds over huge swaths of land—despite his deep knowledge of grafting. Using this unpredictable method, he spread the glory of apples across thousands of acres in the Northwest territory, barefoot and in rags. At the time, the government offered free land to incentivize settlers to move into the Northwest territory, requiring only that they planted an orchard to stake their claim. He eschewed material comforts yet sought to turn a profit, diligently nurturing the orchards and building fences to protect both the trees and his claim to the land. He sold a great deal of the land he had claimed, but at the time of his death, he still had 1,200 acres of unsold land.

Apple people know that most of us know nothing about their singular obsession and all its rarefied permutations, and that the average person might even find their passion a little odd.

They can't help themselves, though—apples are fascinating, and apple people are compelled to spread the word. This may come in the form of growing a dizzying variety of apples for weekend farm goers to pick themselves, compelling them to acknowledge the limitless potential of the apple. Or it could be showing off photos, like a proud parent, of a wild apple tree in an abandoned field, before offering a sip of its effervescent nectar. Or maybe it's pretending you just happened across a pie shop while you were out walking your apples, hoping that a baker there will appreciate them. Whatever the case, when you help someone fall in love with apples, you help them fall in love with life itself.

CLASSIC APPLE PIE

Makes one 9-inch (23-cm) pie

1½ pounds (680 g) peeled and sliced apples (see Note)

2 teaspoons lemon juice

2 tablespoons packed light brown sugar

⅓ cup (65 g) granulated sugar

1 tablespoon plus 2 teaspoons tapioca starch

Scant ½ teaspoon ground cinnamon

⅛ teaspoon ground nutmeg

Scant ½ teaspoon salt

1 recipe Butter Pastry Dough (page 38), bottom crust prepared to make a double-crust pie (see pages 50 and 53)

Egg Wash (page 56)

Note: Some of my favorite baking apples, in no particular order, are Newtown Pippin, Arkansas Black, Northern Spy, Bramley's Seedling, and Stayman Winesap.

THIS IS MY CLASSIC APPLE PIE. BAKED IN A BUTTER CRUST AND served warm, it will change the mind of anyone who thinks apple pie is boring, basic, or dull. The flavor is apple-y above all else—not overly spiced or sweetened. As long as you use nice, firm apples, the texture will have a little bite and will be neither dry nor runny. It has a bit of extra salt relative to other fruit fillings, which rounds out the flavor and enhances the warmth of the spices. In short, this is a pie that will win a person over. I prefer it with a classic butter crust, warm, with Vanilla Bean Ice Cream (page 229).

Preheat the oven to 400°F (205°C).

In a large bowl, combine the sliced apples and lemon juice, then add the brown sugar and stir to combine. In a small bowl, whisk together the granulated sugar, tapioca starch, cinnamon, nutmeg, and salt, making sure that the starch is evenly dispersed. Pour the sugar-spice mixture over the apples and toss to coat. Pour the filling into the bottom crust, making sure to scrape the entire contents from the sides of the bowl into the pie.

Top the pie with the top crust according to the instructions on page 53. Brush the top crust with the egg wash. Place the pie on a baking sheet to collect any juices that bubble over. Bake for 20 minutes, then reduce the heat to 375°F (190°C) and continue to bake for 40 minutes more, or until the filling has been bubbling for at least 10 minutes.

Transfer the pie to a cooling rack and allow to cool for at least 30 minutes before serving to make slicing and serving easier. Serve warm or at room temperature. The pie will keep for up to 3 days at room temperature.

Cranberry Apple Variation:
Stir ⅓ cup (30 g) fresh cranberries into the apple mixture before pouring the filling into the bottom crust.

MAPLE-BUTTER APPLE PIE

Makes one 9-inch (23-cm) pie

3 tablespoons unsalted butter

3 tablespoons maple syrup

⅛ teaspoon ground nutmeg

⅛ teaspoon ground cardamom

⅛ teaspoon ground allspice

¼ teaspoon ground cinnamon

1½ pounds (680 g) peeled and sliced apples (see Note on page 98)

2 teaspoons lemon juice

⅓ cup (65 g) sugar

2 tablespoons tapioca starch

¼ teaspoon salt

1 bottom crust, crimped (½ recipe any crust type; see pages 50 and 52)

1 recipe Cornmeal-Pecan Crumb, made with black walnuts in place of pecans (page 58)

WHILE MY OTHER APPLE PIE RECIPE IS AS SIMPLE AS CAN BE, THIS recipe uses browned butter, a variety of spices, and the woody, caramelized flavor of maple syrup to make an apple pie with layers of flavor that is perfect on a chilly winter day.

Preheat the oven to 400°F (205°C).

In a lightly colored, large saucepan (so that you can see the color of the butter as it cooks—white enamel or stainless steel both work well), melt the butter over medium heat. After the butter melts and begins to bubble, heat for 5 to 10 minutes more, stirring with a wooden spoon, until the butter browns. When the butter is sufficiently browned, small chunks of toasty brown caramelized milk solids will have formed, and the rest of the butter will have a deep, golden-brown hue. Remove from the heat and whisk in the maple syrup, nutmeg, cardamom, allspice, and cinnamon. Add the apple slices and stir to coat. Stir in the lemon juice.

In a small bowl, whisk together the sugar, tapioca starch, and salt, making sure that the starch is evenly dispersed. Pour the sugar mixture over the apples and stir to coat. Pour the filling into the bottom crust, making sure to scrape the entire contents from the sides of the pan into the pie.

Top the filling with the crumb according to the instructions on page 58. Place the pie on a baking sheet to collect any juices that bubble over and bake for 20 minutes, then reduce the heat to 375°F (190°C) and continue to bake for 40 minutes more, or until the filling has been bubbling for at least 10 minutes.

Transfer the pie to a cooling rack and allow to cool for at least 1 hour before serving. Serve warm or at room temperature. The pie will keep for up to 3 days at room temperature.

STONE FRUIT AND BERRY PIES

Each recipe variation makes enough filling for one 9-inch (23-cm) pie

Your preferred Stone Fruit & Berry Filling ingredients (see page 104)

1 bottom crust (½ recipe) or 1 recipe any crust type, depending on if you want a crumb or streusel topping or a top crust (see pages 50, 53, 54–55, and 57–59)

1 recipe streusel or crumb topping (see pages 57–59), if using

Egg Wash (page 56), if using a top crust

Note: Make sure to slice your stone fruit over a bowl to collect the juices, and include the juice in the final weight. (Weigh the empty bowl first so you don't count its weight in the total.)

MANY VARIETIES OF STONE FRUIT AND BERRIES TEND TO COME INTO season at the same time. When you put them together in a pie, they offer an intriguing contrast of flavors, textures, and colors. These pies can be made with any kind of crust and/or crumb topping, so there are dozens of variations available to you. See page 104 for my favorite combinations.

Preheat the oven to 400°F (205°C).

In a large bowl, combine the fruits with the lemon juice. In a small bowl, whisk together the sugar, tapioca starch, and salt, making sure that the starch is evenly dispersed. Pour the sugar mixture over the fruit and gently stir to coat. Pour all the filling into the bottom crust, making sure to scrape the entire contents from the sides of the bowl into the pie.

Top the filling with a streusel or crumb according to the instructions on pages 57–59, if using, or top with a top crust according to the instructions on pages 53 or 54–55. Brush the top crust, if using, with the egg wash. Place the pie on a baking sheet to collect any juices that bubble over. Bake for 20 minutes, then reduce the heat to 375°F (190°C) and continue to bake for 40 minutes more, or until the filling has been bubbling for at least 10 minutes.

Transfer the pie to a cooling rack and allow to cool for at least 45 minutes before serving. Serve warm or at room temperature. The pie will keep for up to 3 days at room temperature.

APRICOT-RED CURRANT FILLING

Bright red, bracingly tart currants add a bright contrast of flavor and color to sweet, mellow apricots. Since apricots are so small, it's not worth the trouble of removing the skin. Having the skin intact actually helps the slices hold their shape.

1¼ pounds (570 g) sliced apricots, plus juices (see Note on page 102)

4 ounces (115 g) red currants

2 teaspoons lemon juice

½ cup (100 g) sugar

¼ cup (35 g) tapioca starch

¼ teaspoon salt

PEACH-GOOSEBERRY FILLING

Gooseberries are more popular in Europe than in the United States, due to the same unnecessary ban that for so many years prohibited the cultivation of black currants. They can be used in various states of ripeness. When they're green, they are super tart, and when they develop a blush they've ripened and sweetened up a bit. Depending on your taste, either works well in this recipe, in which they lend an unusual, almost tropical tartness to the filling.

1 pound (455 g) peach slices (skin removed), plus juices (see Note on page 102)

8 ounces (225 g) halved gooseberries

1 tablespoon lemon juice

⅓ cup plus 1 tablespoon (80 g) sugar

⅓ cup (45 g) tapioca starch

¼ teaspoon salt

SHIRO PLUM AND BLACK RASPBERRY FILLING

In this combination, it's the berries that are mellow and the plums that provide the vibrant acidity. A lot of the shiro plum's flavor is in and near the skin, so I recommend keeping the skin intact.

1 pound (455 g) sliced shiro plums, plus juices (see Note on page 102)

8 ounces (225 g) black raspberries

1 tablespoon lemon juice

⅓ cup plus 1 tablespoon (80 g) sugar

⅓ cup (45 g) tapioca starch

¼ teaspoon salt

BLACKBERRY-NECTARINE FILLING

Fresh ripe blackberries, with their deep dark color and appealing tartness, combine so beautifully with juicy yellow nectarines.

1 pound (455 g) sliced nectarines, plus juices (see Note on page 102)

8 ounces (225 g) blackberries

2 teaspoons lemon juice

⅓ cup plus 1 tablespoon (80 g) sugar

⅓ cup (45 g) tapioca starch

¼ teaspoon salt

MINCE PIE

Makes two 9-inch (23-cm) pies

½ cup (70 g) dried black currants (not Zante currants; see Note on page 80)

½ cup (75 g) raisins

½ cup (120 ml) brandy

½ cup (120 ml) pommeau, port, or sweet sherry

½ cup (1 stick/115 g) unsalted butter

¼ teaspoon ground cinnamon

½ teaspoon ground allspice

¼ teaspoon ground nutmeg

¼ teaspoon ground cloves

½ teaspoon salt

1 cup (220 g) packed brown sugar

1 pound (455 g) peeled apples, cut into ½-inch (12-mm) cubes

½ cup (80 g) halved sour cherries

¼ Meyer lemon, seeds removed, minced with its peel

2 recipes of any crust type, bottom crusts prepared to make a double-crust pies (see pages 50 and 53)

Egg Wash (page 56)

MINCE PIE IS A TRADITIONAL HOLIDAY DESSERT IN THE UK AND New England, where it is known as mincemeat pie. It is made with apples, dried and candied fruits, and a nice splash of booze. This meatless mince filling is meant to be made ahead and aged before baking it into a pie, so that the flavors can deepen and meld. Since this process is somewhat time-consuming, I find it's more efficient to make two pies, and because of this the recipe yields enough filling for two—make one pie for yourself and give the other as a gift.

One Christmas, I accidentally left a box of mince pie under some gift boxes and found it a few weeks later. It was still good! The brandy and butter are both excellent preservatives. And try it with the Holiday Custard Sauce (see page 227). While you can keep extra filling for a year in the freezer, and your baked pie may actually last quite a bit longer than a week at room temperature, the pie is at its very best when eaten within a few days.

In a medium bowl, soak the currants and raisins in the brandy and pommeau for roughly 1 hour while you make the rest of the filling.

In a lightly colored, large saucepan (so that you can see the color of the butter as it cooks—white enamel or stainless steel both work well), melt the butter over medium heat. After the butter melts and begins to bubble, heat for 5 to 10 minutes more, stirring with a wooden spoon, until the butter browns. When the butter is sufficiently browned, small chunks of toasty brown caramelized milk solids will have formed, and the rest of the butter will have a deep, golden-brown hue. Remove from the heat and whisk in the cinnamon, allspice, nutmeg, cloves, and salt. Allow to sit for about a minute to bring out the essence of the spices. Whisk in the brown sugar, then add the apples, cherries, and minced Meyer lemon and stir to coat. Return the pan to low heat and cook for 5 to 10 minutes, or until the apples have softened slightly. Remove from the heat.

Continued

Add the soaked fruit with the liquid to the fruit-butter mixture and stir well. Divide the mixture into two large glass jars with lids. Allow to sit overnight at room temperature, then at least a week in the fridge and up to 2 months to allow the flavors to meld before baking. The longer the aging time, the more melded the brandy, spice, and citrus flavors become.

When you are ready to make the pies, preheat the oven to 400°F (205°C).

Pour the filings into the bottom crusts. Top the pies with the top crusts according to the instructions on page 53. Brush the top crusts with the egg wash. Alternatively, you can make one pie after aging the filling for a week and continue to age the other jar of filling for up to 2 months before using it in a pie. Place the pie(s) on a baking sheet to collect any juices that bubble over. Bake for 20 minutes, then reduce the heat to 375°F (190°C) and continue to bake for 40 minutes more, or until the filling has been bubbling for at least 10 minutes.

Transfer the pie(s) to a cooling rack and allow to cool for at least 1 hour before serving. Serve warm or at room temperature. The pie(s) will keep for 1 week or more at room temperature.

Note: Prepare the dough and the egg wash on the day that you plan on making the pie, or use dough that you've prepared earlier and frozen, allowing time for it to defrost. If you would like to make a Savory Mincemeat Pie to serve at your holiday dinner, see page 206 for a recipe that includes meat.

CHILLED
PIES

Imagine: It's late at night and you are in a diner. Your spoon is greasy, your belly is full, and yet . . . You see a rotating refrigerated display, designed to prevent you from leaving without first succumbing to your sweet tooth. What do you see inside? I have a few guesses. Jiggly lemon curd piled high with toasted peaks of meringue? Deep dark-chocolate custard, starkly contrasted with fluffy whipped cream? Slices of cheesecake with bright red cherries dripping down the sides?

Humble and *rustic* are words often used to describe pie, but the recipes in this section are anything but. Vibrant berry tarts, sweet-tart key lime, and jiggly chiffons—these are arguably the most decadent of pies. They are showstoppers, worthy of a celebration.

A handful of these recipes can be topped with either a quick and easy Vanilla Whipped Cream (page 231) or a super-silky Vanilla Sea Salt Meringue (page 231), which is more laborious but very impressive. With the exception of the cheesecake, all of them can be made in a gluten-free version.

COCONUT CREAM PIE

Makes one 9-inch (23-cm) pie

½ cup (45 g) unsweetened shredded coconut

¼ cup (60 ml) coconut water

⅔ cup (135 g) sugar

2 tablespoons cornstarch

⅛ teaspoon salt

1 egg

3 egg yolks

⅔ cup (165 ml) heavy cream

⅔ cup (165 ml) whole milk

½ teaspoon vanilla

1 bottom crust of Coconut Crust (page 48), blind-baked (½ recipe; see pages 50 and 60)

Vanilla Sea Salt Meringue (page 231) or Vanilla Whipped Cream (page 231)

¼ cup (20 g) coconut flakes

IF YOU WANT PURE, NUTTY COCONUT FLAVOR, ORGANIC unsweeted shredded coconut is superior to the sweetened shredded coconut you typically find in the baking aisle of the grocery store. However, due to its lack of moisture, it needs to be reconstituted somewhat before it's used in this filling. To do that, as well as to add even more coconut flavor, I use coconut water. The resulting pie has the rich dairy flavor that I look for in a cream pie, but with plenty of nutty coconut flavor. It can be topped with Vanilla Whipped Cream as shown here for a quick and easy topping, or for a more elegant approach try the Vanilla Sea Salt Meringue. For the crust, use the Coconut Crust variation of either the Butter Pastry Dough or Gluten-Free Pastry Dough.

In a small container with a watertight lid, combine the shredded coconut and coconut water. Tighten the lid and shake the container to moisten the shredded coconut.

In a medium saucepan, whisk together the sugar, cornstarch, and salt. Whisk in the egg and egg yolks to form a paste. Gradually whisk in the cream, then whisk in the milk. Cook over medium heat, whisking constantly, until you feel the pudding start to thicken on the bottom of the pan, about 10 minutes. Reduce the heat to low and trade your whisk for a rubber spatula. Continue stirring with the spatula, scraping the sides and bottom of the pan to prevent burning. Cook for 10 to 15 minutes more, or until the pudding has bubbled for about 2 minutes and has thickened. Remove from the heat and stir in the vanilla and moistened coconut until the coconut water is completely incorporated into the pudding.

Pour the hot filling into the blind-baked crust, making sure to scrape the entire contents from the sides of the pan into the pie. Use the spatula to ease the pudding up the sides of the shell, leaving about ½ inch (12 mm) of the crust exposed on the outer edge. This helps the crust stay intact when slicing.

Continued

If topping with meringue:

Dip a spoon in hot water. Pile the meringue on top of the pudding, using the back of the hot, wet spoon to create a wavy texture with peaks and valleys. Sprinkle the coconut flakes over the meringue.

Set the oven rack so that when the pie is on it, the very top of the pie is 3 to 5 inches (7.5 to 12 cm) from the heating element.

Turn the broiler on high. When the heat is in full effect, place the pie under the broiler and set a timer for 1 minute. Broiler heat varies wildly from oven to oven, so keep a close eye on the pie for the entire time it is under the broiler. Heat until the peaks and coconut flakes turn golden brown, anywhere from 1 to 3 minutes, depending on your oven.

Allow the pie to cool at room temperature for 30 minutes, then transfer the pie to the fridge for about 4 hours. To serve, slice with a hot, wet knife in order to avoid dragging the meringue.

If topping with whipped cream:

Chill the pie in the fridge for 1 hour, or until the surface of the pudding is cool to the touch.

While the pie cools, toast the coconut flakes: In a pan on low heat, stir the coconut flakes constantly to prevent burning, until the coconut is fragrant and the edges are a deep golden color. Set aside to cool to room temperature.

Transfer the whipped cream to a pastry bag with a round tip and pipe dollops onto the pudding, starting at the outer edge and working your way to the center. Sprinkle with the toasted coconut flakes. Refrigerate for 3 hours before serving.

The pie is best eaten the same day, but it will keep for up to 3 days, covered, in the fridge.

CHOCOLATE CREAM PIE

Makes one 9-inch (23-cm) pie

¾ cup (150 g) sugar

3 tablespoons unsweetened cocoa

1 tablespoon plus 2 teaspoons cornstarch

⅛ teaspoon salt

2 eggs

1 egg yolk

¾ cup (180 ml) heavy cream

¾ cup (180 ml) whole milk

½ teaspoon vanilla

3 tablespoons (35 g) chopped dark chocolate

1 bottom crust, blind-baked (½ recipe any crust type; see pages 50 and 60)

Vanilla Sea Salt Meringue (page 231) or Vanilla Whipped Cream (page 231)

¼ cup (35 g) dark chocolate shavings or gilded chocolate flakes (optional; see Note on page 115)

THIS PIE HAS A DEEP, DARK CHOCOLATE FILLING AND IS RICH without being too sweet. It can be topped with Vanilla Whipped Cream as shown here, or the Vanilla Sea Salt Meringue, which has a subtle saltiness and silky texture that complements the chocolate beautifully.

In a medium saucepan, sift the sugar, cocoa, cornstarch, and salt. Whisk in the eggs, egg yolk, and half of the cream. Gradually whisk in the remaining cream, then whisk in the milk. Cook over medium heat, whisking constantly, until you feel the pudding start to thicken on the bottom of the pan, about 10 minutes. Reduce the heat to low and trade your whisk for a rubber spatula. Continue stirring with the spatula, scraping the sides and bottom of the pan to prevent burning. Cook for 10 to 15 minutes more, or until the pudding has bubbled for about 2 minutes and has thickened. Remove from the heat and stir in the vanilla and chopped chocolate until the chocolate has melted and the mixture is completely smooth.

Pour the hot pudding into the blind-baked pie crust, making sure to scrape the entire contents from the sides of the pan into the pie. Use the spatula to ease the pudding up the sides of the shell, leaving about ½ inch (12 mm) of the crust exposed on the outer edge.

If topping with meringue:
Pile the meringue on top of the pudding, using the back of a hot, wet spoon to create a wavy texture with peaks and valleys, or transfer the meringue to a pastry bag fitted with a fluted or round tip and pipe it on.

Set the oven rack so that when the pie is on it, the very top of the pie is 3 to 5 inches (7.5 to 12 cm) from the heating element.

Turn the broiler on high. When the heat is in full effect, place the pie under the broiler and set a timer for 1 minute. Broiler heat varies wildly from oven to oven, so keep a close eye on the pie for the entire

Continued

time it is under the broiler. Heat until the peaks of the meringue turn golden brown, anywhere from 1 to 3 minutes, depending on your oven.

Transfer the pie to the fridge for 4 hours or until cooled completely.

Before serving, sprinkle the chocolate shavings, if using, over the meringue. To serve, slice with a hot, wet knife in order to avoid dragging the meringue.

If topping with whipped cream:
Chill the pie in the fridge for 1 hour, or until the surface of the pudding is cool to the touch. Transfer the whipped cream to a pastry bag with a round tip and pipe the whipped cream onto the pudding, making a mound of whipped cream in the center to build volume, then piping the rest over the pudding in a spiral shape. Sprinkle with the chocolate shavings or gilded chocolate flakes, if using. Refrigerate for 3 hours before serving.

The pie is best eaten the same day, but it will keep up to 3 days, covered, in the fridge.

Note: To make gilded chocolate flakes, melt ⅓ cup (60 g) chopped dark chocolate in a double boiler. Use an offset spatula to spread the chocolate in a thin layer on a silicone mat or waxed paper. Gently transfer 4 sheets edible gold leaf onto the layer of melted chocolate. Chill completely in the fridge before peeling the chocolate off the mat and breaking it into small flakes.

SPRING CORDIAL PIE

Makes one 9-inch (23-cm) pie

For the lemon-elderflower filling and assembly:

1 cup (200 g) sugar

⅓ cup (45 g) cornstarch

¼ teaspoon salt

3 egg yolks (use the whites to make the meringue)

1 egg

½ cup (120 ml) elderflower cordial or elderflower liqueur, such as St. Germain

¾ cup (180 ml) freshly squeezed lemon juice, from 4 to 6 lemons

3 tablespoons cold unsalted butter

1 bottom crust, blind-baked (½ recipe any crust type; see pages 50 and 60)

For the elderflower meringue:

½ cup (120 ml) egg whites (equivalent of 3 large egg whites), at room temperature

½ teaspoon cream of tartar

¼ cup (60 ml) elderflower cordial or liqueur, such as St. Germain

¾ cup (150 g) sugar

¼ teaspoon vanilla

Pinch of salt

Edible flower or micro-flower petals (optional)

WHEN THE TINY WHITE FLOWERS OF THE ELDER TREE BLOOM IN late spring, their ethereal scent fills the air and attracts honeybees and humans alike. Elderflowers are often enjoyed with lemon juice in the form of a cordial, which is the inspiration for this pie. It's beautiful topped with edible flower petals or micro-flowers. The lemon-elderflower filling can also be used in Berry Dream Pie (page 141), or anywhere you'd use lemon curd. It's fantastic over Greek yogurt!

Make the lemon-elderflower filling and assemble the pie:
In a medium bowl, whisk together the sugar, cornstarch, and salt, making sure that the starch is evenly dispersed. Whisk in the egg yolks, whole egg, cordial, and ¼ cup (60 ml) water. Whisk in the lemon juice, then pass the mixture through a sieve into a small saucepan.

Place the pan over medium heat and stir constantly with a rubber spatula, scraping the sides and bottom of the pan to prevent burning. When the filling starts thickening on the bottom of the pan, reduce the heat to the lowest setting. Continue stirring constantly until all the filling has thickened but is still a pourable consistency, about 10 minutes. Remove from the heat and add the butter. Stir until the butter has melted and is completely incorporated into the filling. The filling can be used as a lemon curd and stored for up to 1 week in an airtight container in the fridge.

Pour the hot filling into the blind-baked crust, making sure to scrape the entire contents from the sides of the pan into the pie. Use the spatula to ease the pudding up the sides of the shell, leaving about ½ inch (12 mm) of the crust exposed on the outer edge.

Place in the fridge and chill the pie for at least 1 hour, or until the surface of the pudding is cool to the touch.

Continued

Make the elderflower meringue:

In either a stand mixer with a whisk attachment or in a large bowl with a hand-held mixer, beat the egg whites and cream of tartar on high until white and foamy.

In a saucepan, combine the cordial and sugar over medium heat and stir until the sugar has completely dissolved and the syrup begins to bubble. Remove from the heat.

With the mixer running, pour the hot syrup in a thin stream into the foamy egg whites. Continue beating until the meringue holds the pattern of the whisk as it spins. The texture should be voluminous but still silky. Add the vanilla and salt and beat just until combined.

Pile the meringue on top of the filling, using the back of a hot, wet spoon to create decorative peaks, if desired.

Set the oven rack so that when the pie is on it, the very top of the pie is 3 to 5 inches (7.5 to 12 cm) from the heating element.

Turn the broiler on high. When the heat is in full effect, place the pie under the broiler and set a timer for 1 minute. Broiler heat varies wildly from oven to oven, so keep a close eye on the pie for the entire time it is under the broiler. Heat until the peaks of the meringue turn golden brown, anywhere from 1 to 3 minutes, depending on your oven.

Transfer the pie to the fridge for 4 hours or until cooled completely. Before serving, sprinkle with the micro-flowers or flower petals, if using. To serve, slice with a hot, wet knife in order to avoid dragging the meringue. The pie will keep for up to 4 days, covered, in the fridge.

COFFEE CREAM PIE

Makes one 9-inch (23-cm) pie

For the coffee pudding and assembly:

⅔ cup (135 g) sugar

2 tablespoons cornstarch

¾ teaspoon instant espresso powder

⅛ teaspoon salt

1 egg

2 egg yolks

⅔ cup (165 ml) heavy cream

⅔ cup (165 ml) whole milk

1 teaspoon vanilla

1 bottom crust, blind-baked (½ recipe any crust type; see pages 50 and 60)

For the coffee whipped cream:

⅓ cup (40 g) confectioners' sugar

¾ teaspoon instant espresso powder

Pinch of salt

1½ cups (360 ml) heavy cream

½ teaspoon vanilla

Ground cinnamon, for sprinkling

WHEN I WAS A KID, I WAS IN THE ENVIABLE POSITION OF GROWING up in a bakery with pies, cookies, and pastries that I could snatch straight from the pan. But I always tended to crave things we didn't make, like ice cream—and especially coffee ice cream, which my dad sometimes got for me as a special treat. I loved how the sweet creaminess tempered the dark, roasty coffee flavor. Now I drink my coffee black, but I'm still a sucker for creamy coffee desserts, so I set out to re-create the flavor of coffee ice cream in the form of a pie. This pie is sure to please anyone who enjoys an affogato, Vietnamese coffee, or tiramisu.

Make the coffee pudding and assemble the pie:
In a medium saucepan, whisk together the sugar, cornstarch, espresso powder, and salt. Whisk in the egg and egg yolks to form a paste. Gradually whisk in the cream, then whisk in the milk. Cook over medium heat, whisking constantly, until you feel the pudding start to thicken on the bottom of the pan, about 10 minutes. Reduce the heat to low and trade your whisk for a rubber spatula. Continue stirring with the spatula, scraping the sides and bottom of the pan to prevent burning. Cook for 10 to 15 minutes more, or until the pudding has bubbled for about 2 minutes and has thickened. Remove from the heat and add the vanilla, stirring until smooth.

Pour the hot pudding into the blind-baked crust, making sure to scrape the entire contents from the sides of the pan into the pie. Use the spatula to ease the pudding up the sides of the shell, leaving about ½ inch (12 mm) of the crust exposed on the outer edge.

Place in the fridge and chill the pie for at least 1 hour, or until the surface of the pudding is cool to the touch.

Continued

Make the coffee whipped cream:

Sift the confectioners' sugar into the bowl of a stand mixer or a large bowl, then whisk in the espresso powder and salt. Pour in the heavy cream and vanilla. Using the whisk attachment or a hand-held mixer, beat on high until the cream is voluminous and can still hold its shape but is smooth.

Transfer the coffee whipped cream to a pastry bag with a round tip and pipe dollops onto the pudding, starting at the outer edge and working your way to the center. Put the pie in the fridge for another 3 hours to cool completely before serving. Sprinkle very lightly with cinnamon just before serving.

The pie is best eaten the same day but it will keep for up to 3 days, covered, in the fridge.

Note: Coffee and pie are natural companions. When we started our Lower East Side shop we sold two items: pie and coffee. The duo makes an ideal breakfast or a late-night pick-me-up. And no, it's not overkill to have a cup of coffee with your Coffee Cream Pie!

BANANA CREAM PIE

Makes one 9-inch (23-cm) pie

½ cup (100 g) sugar

1 tablespoon plus 1 teaspoon
   cornstarch

⅛ teaspoon salt

1 egg

2 egg yolks

½ cup (120 ml) heavy cream

½ cup (120 ml) whole milk

1 teaspoon vanilla

1 bottom crust, blind-baked
   (½ recipe any crust type; see
   pages 50 and 60)

2 cups (480 ml) cold water

1 tablespoon salt

1 tablespoon lemon juice

2 medium bananas, slightly underripe

Vanilla Whipped Cream (page 231)

AS MUCH AS I HAVE A SOFT SPOT FOR THE CLASSIC BANANA CREAM pie, which is typically made with instant banana pudding and store-bought vanilla wafers, I'm not one for artificial ingredients. Instead, I make a luscious and simple vanilla pudding and use fresh bananas, paired with a crisp and flaky butter crust. For a more unusual take, make this recipe with a sesame Seeded Crust (page 48).

In a medium saucepan, whisk together the sugar, cornstarch, and salt. Whisk in the egg and egg yolks to form a paste. Gradually whisk in the cream, then whisk in the milk. Cook over medium heat, whisking constantly, until you feel the pudding start to thicken on the bottom of the pan, about 10 minutes. Reduce the heat to low and trade your whisk for a rubber spatula. Continue stirring with the spatula, scraping the sides and bottom of the pan to prevent burning. Cook for 10 to 15 minutes more, or until the pudding has bubbled for about 2 minutes and has thickened. Remove from the heat and whisk in the vanilla until smooth.

Pour the hot pudding into the blind-baked crust, making sure to scrape the entire contents from the sides of the pan into the pie. Use the spatula to ease the pudding up the sides of the shell, leaving about ½ inch (12 mm) of the crust exposed on the outer edge. Allow the filling to cool at room temperature.

Meanwhile, in a medium bowl, combine the water, salt, and lemon juice. Slice the bananas into ½-inch (12-mm) pieces and put them in the water bath. Drain the bananas with a sieve, shaking the water off, but don't rinse—the salt and lemon will help prevent browning. Arrange the banana slices in the top of the pudding, pressing them in slightly.

Transfer the pie to the fridge and chill until it is cool to the touch, about 30 minutes. Transfer the whipped cream to a pastry bag with a round tip and pipe dollops onto the pudding, starting at the outer edge and working your way to the center. Refrigerate for 4 hours before serving. The pie is best eaten the same day, but it will keep up to 3 days, covered, in the fridge.

LOVE, LEMONS, AND LIMES

The first time I visited my now-husband Robert's parents, Sylvia and Bob, at their home in South Central Los Angeles, we already had a business plan in the works for our first pie shop. It would be an understatement to say my late father-in-law was enthusiastic about the idea. He had a massive sweet tooth and a scheming entrepreneurial spirit, so the concept of a pie enterprise hit all the right notes. He got so much vicarious pleasure and pride out of our plans that he created a celebratory signature for the end of all his texts. It read, "PETEE'S PIES in NYC!!!" sandwiched between all the fruit emojis.

Having grown up in Virginia, I was enchanted by the proliferation of citrus trees in Bob and Sylvia's neighborhood. They didn't have any lemon trees in their yard, but several of their neighbors did.

At some point during our visit I told Bob that I'd love to work on my lemon meringue pie recipe and asked if he thought any of his neighbors would spare some lemons. He hastily answered in the affirmative, grabbed a fruit basket, and told me he'd be right back. Not long after, Sylvia wandered into the kitchen with Robert, wondering about Bob's whereabouts. I told her that he went to ask the neighbors for some lemons, not anticipating the look of confusion and concern that fell over her face. Robert seemed incredulous as well, saying: "The neighbors? He doesn't know the neighbors!" I thought that was an odd thing to say about someone who had lived in the same neighborhood his entire life, but Bob had a reputation for being mischievous, territorial, and insular—fiercely proud of his family, but perhaps not the best neighbor material.

Perfectly ripe Meyer lemons ready to be picked on Garcia Farm, with the Santa Ana Mountains in the background.

We walked out the back door to see Bob perched precariously on top of a ladder that he had leaned against the corner of their fence. He had bypassed any interaction with his backyard neighbors and filled the basket from an overburdened branch of their tree. He dismounted the ladder and with great satisfaction presented me with his bounty—far more round, gigantic lemons than I could use in a single pie. I thanked him and got straight to work. The ensuing pie was an overwhelming success (despite the fact that Bob couldn't manage to wait for it to cool before slicing into it), all the more because of the freshness of the hard-won lemons.

I've been back to Southern California many times since then, and the smell and sight of citrus trees will never fail to enchant me. Citrus juice—especially lemon—will always be a staple in my pie recipes, regardless of my steadfast support for local agriculture. Just as it's worthwhile to seek out responsible, independent farmers at your local market, it's a great pleasure to do so when you travel as well, or to find an independent source for one of your staple ingredients that can't be grown near you. For me, one such example of this is Garcia Organic Farm in Deluz, California.

Garcia Organic Farm has been the chosen work of Juan Garcia, and by extension his family, for three decades. Juan began working for a nearby citrus farmer as an eighteen-year-old immigrant from Mexico, around the same time he married his wife, Coco, but he was so slight and sweet-faced that his employer initially suspected he was no more than fourteen and doubted his ability to keep up with the rest of his staff. He worked hard and steadily, and thus proved his worth to both his employer and Coco's dubious parents.

After working in the citrus groves for nearly twenty years, he bought ten acres of his own, then gradually added on neighboring parcels of land as they went up for sale. Now his farm spreads out to around thirty acres, much of it achingly steep, but to this day, he has never stopped working for his original employer as well—in fact, his expert role of breeding and nurturing new plants in the nursery remains indispensable for them.

Since another job takes up much of his time, Juan's progeny are important contributors to the success of Garcia Organic Farm. All of his adult sons, and some of their spouses as well, work for the farm in one way or another. When I reached out one winter about visiting, it was Lety Garcia, wife of Juan and Coco's son Armando, who responded and gave me and my family a tour. In addition to handling inquiries such as mine, she transports the produce to their biggest market, the organic Santa Monica Farmers Market, and along the way drops some off at the airport to be transported to New York by Baldor, a food distributor.

Since anyone in Southern California can grow a lemon or lime tree in their backyard, the

Garcias stand out by growing all manner of exotic citrus, from tiny kumquats and finger limes to squishy sweet Satsuma oranges and giant pithy pomelos. In addition to their astounding assortment of citrus, they grow a handful of avocado varieties, exotic mulberries, guavas, cherimoyas, guanabanas (soursops), passion fruit, bananas, and even a few macadamia nut trees on their property.

Aside from the impressive variety of their produce, another thing that makes the Garcias special is that they do everything organically. This means using beneficial insects to fight parasitic insects that would compromise their crops, and occasionally eradicating a section of trees in order to prevent the spread of a disease, which they had to do with their makrut lime trees shortly before our visit.

Perhaps it's fitting that when visiting such a farm, we came in three generations—me and Robert, our kids Eloisa and Alejo, and my mother-in-law, Sylvia. I was carrying Alejo, and Robert was taking photos, when Eloisa expressed her exhaustion at walking up and down the steep hills, and Lety picked her up without a second thought. She carried her the rest of the time without breaking a sweat, and despite often being finicky and shy around new people, Eloisa had no complaints. Lety has that effect on people— she makes you comfortable right away and radiates positivity, which I think is a big part of what makes their stand the most popular at the Santa Monica Farmers Market.

After walking us through so many groves and allowing us to fill up bag after bag of produce, much of which I'd only seen and never tasted, Lety introduced us to Juan at the farm's sorting and packing building. He ran the avocado sorting machine for us, which sorted the avocados by size for the market, and showed us the bushel boxes of every imaginable size and shape of citrus.

After that, we were invited to meet Coco for lunch up at their house. It was built on the very highest point on the property, and the walls of the living space were covered with framed family photos spanning four generations. Coco made us a simple and perfect meal of tostadas with sliced avocado and nectar-sweet satsuma juice over ice. It was a pleasant relief for both Coco and Lety that we could converse casually in Spanish—Coco could be more fluid in her conversation and Lety wasn't required to translate.

Two days later, we visited their stand at the Santa Monica Farmers Market, where Lety was once again overwhelmingly generous with lemons. Between visiting the farm and the market, we'd gathered enough citrus and avocados that we had to borrow an extra suitcase from Sylvia to transport them back to New York! The shock of the cold February air as we deboarded the plane was a little easier to take knowing that we had a suitcase full of California sunshine to enjoy in the coming days.

LEMON MERINGUE PIE

Makes one 9-inch (23-cm) pie

1¼ cups (250 g) sugar

¼ cup (30 g) cornstarch

¼ teaspoon salt

3 egg yolks (use the whites to make the meringue)

1 egg

1 cup plus 2 tablespoons (270 ml) freshly squeezed lemon juice, from about 8 to 10 lemons

3 tablespoons cold unsalted butter

1 bottom crust, blind-baked (½ recipe any crust type—try the Seeded Crust with poppyseeds, page 48; see pages 50 and 60)

Lemon Poppyseed Meringue (page 231)

THE COMBINATION OF SILKY MERINGUE AND TANGY, JIGGLY lemon curd is timeless and practical—the number of yolks in the filling matches the number of whites in the meringue. A poppyseed crust and meringue adds a pleasing texture and a bit more complexity.

In a medium bowl, whisk together the sugar, cornstarch, and salt, making sure that the starch is evenly dispersed. Whisk in the egg yolks, whole egg, and ¼ cup plus 2 tablespoons (90 ml) water. Whisk in the lemon juice, then pass the mixture through a sieve into a small saucepan.

Place the pan over medium heat and stir constantly with a rubber spatula, scraping the sides and bottom of the pan to prevent burning. After about 5 to 8 minutes, when the filling starts thickening on the bottom of the pan, reduce the heat to the lowest setting. Continue stirring constantly, until all the filling has thickened but is still a pourable consistency, about 5 minutes more. Remove from the heat and add the butter. Stir until the butter has melted and is completely incorporated.

Pour the hot filling into the blind-baked crust, making sure to scrape the entire contents from the sides of the pan into the pie. Use the spatula to ease the filling up the sides of the shell, leaving about ½ inch (12 mm) of the crust exposed on the outer edge. Pile the meringue on top of the lemon curd, using the back of a hot, wet spoon to create a wavy texture with peaks and valleys.

Set the oven rack so that when the pie is on it, the very top of the pie is 3 to 5 inches (7.5 to 12 cm) from the heating element. Turn the broiler on high. When the heat is in full effect, place the pie under the broiler and set a timer for 1 minute. Broiler heat varies wildly from oven to oven, so keep a close eye on the pie for the entire time it is under the broiler. Heat until the peaks turn golden brown, anywhere from 1 to 3 minutes, depending on your oven.

Transfer the pie to the fridge for 4 hours or until cooled completely. To serve, slice with a hot, wet knife in order to avoid dragging the meringue. The pie will keep for up to 4 days, covered, in the fridge.

KEY LIME MERINGUE PIE

Makes one 9-inch (23-cm) pie

1¼ cups (300 ml) sweetened condensed milk (equivalent to a 14-ounce/420-ml can, or home-made; see recipe on page 230)

5 egg yolks

½ cup plus 2 tablespoons (150 ml) freshly squeezed lime juice, from about 6 to 7 Persian limes, or 14 to 16 key limes

Zest of 1 key lime or half a Persian lime

1 bottom crust of Coconut Crust (page 48), par-baked (½ recipe; see pages 50 and 60)

Vanilla Sea Salt Meringue (page 231)

SOME PEOPLE INSIST THAT KEY LIME PIE CAN ONLY BE MADE with true key limes. These tiny, super tart, and floral-scented limes originated in Southeast Asia, made their way westward, and were brought to the West Indies and Florida Keys by Spanish explorers. But Persian limes—the standard green variety you get at the grocery store—can also make for a great pie. The key (sorry!) is simply using freshly squeezed lime juice. The coconut crust variation of the butter pastry dough gives this pie an even more tropical vibe.

Preheat the oven to 350°F (175°C).

In a large bowl, whisk together the sweetened condensed milk and egg yolks. Add the lime juice and whisk until smooth. Whisk in the lime zest.

Pour the filling into the par-baked crust, making sure to scrape the entire contents from the sides of the bowl into the pie. Bake for 18 to 20 minutes, or until the outer edges of the pie have solidified, but the center of the pie looks slightly fluid under the surface when the pie is jiggled.

Pile the meringue on top of the pudding, using the back of a hot, wet spoon to create a wavy texture with peaks and valleys, or transfer the meringue to a pastry bag fitted with a fluted tip and pipe it on, starting at the outer edge and working your way to the center.

Set the oven rack so that when the pie is on it, the very top of the pie is 3 to 5 inches (7.5 to 12 cm) from the heating element.

Turn the broiler on high. When the heat is in full effect, place the pie under the broiler and set a timer for 1 minute. Broiler heat varies wildly from oven to oven, so keep a close eye on the pie for the entire time it is under the broiler. Heat until the peaks of the meringue turn golden brown, anywhere from 1 to 3 minutes, depending on your oven.

Transfer the pie to the fridge for 4 hours or until cooled completely. To serve, slice with a hot, wet knife in order to avoid dragging the meringue. The pie will keep for up to 5 days, covered, in the fridge.

NESSELRODE, A NEW YORK YEARNING

My husband, Robert, and I discovered Nesselrode pie while poring over the New York City Public Library's menu archives shortly after opening our shop. In our search for bygone pies, we saw endless varieties of cream pies, custard pies, and fruit pies à la mode—after all, up through the mid-twentieth century it was unusual for an American restaurant to not feature pie for dessert. Most of them were familiar flavors, but a mysterious name, Nesselrode, kept popping up on menu after menu. What an odd and undescriptive name for a pie! The name then turned up in emails from hopeful customers on behalf of their elderly parents, pleading with me to supply them with a pie to satisfy a very specific nostalgic craving. Curious, I looked further into the history of this pie, which was previously unknown to me, despite having grown up in a world of pie.

It turns out that before Nesselrode was reinvented as a pie, it was a popular ice pudding enjoyed in affluent homes and dining establishments across Europe, England, and eventually New York City. And, like so many of the desserts that capture our curiosity, its true origins are by turns confidently stated and hotly contested.

If you do a deep dive into Nesselrode history, you may see the term attributed to Marie-Antoine Carême. Sometimes referred to as the world's first celebrity chef, he was able to imbue his vocation with a great deal of cachet and prestige. In the first edition of his book, *Le Cuisinier Parisien*, Carême published a recipe called Chestnut Pudding, with Rum. It was a boiled pudding, one of many that were made in that era. Later, his colleague known only as Monni created an iced chestnut rum pudding and named it after his employer, a Russian count named Karl von Nesselrode.

In a subsequent edition of his book, Carême included a version of Monni's iced pudding, insisting that his boiled chestnut pudding was Monni's inspiration—simultaneously giving and taking credit for the invention of Nesselrode pudding. He chose to call the recipe French Chestnut Pudding instead. He was fed up with glorious French dishes being given foreign attributions and wrote in the recipe's introduction, "I am always astonished that we have the habit of giving foreign denominations to the excellent dishes we compose; why this, when the French cuisine is recognized [as the] universal cuisine?"

Issues of intellectual property aside, the Nesselrode pudding became perhaps the most popular ice pudding around, and it was an extremely decadent dessert in an era without refrigeration. Typically made of a custard of pureed chestnuts, cream, vanilla sugar syrup, maraschino liqueur (a clear, sweet liqueur that isn't particularly cherry flavored, despite being made from Marasca cherries), candied citron, and raisins, the pudding uses Italian meringue, which is folded in to lighten the texture before being poured into a mold and frozen. (One notable exception is a version made by Emma Darwin—yes, Charles Darwin's wife—with almonds, crumbled macarons, and brandy.) Its popularity endured for decades, and later versions evolved to include rum

or brandy in place of the maraschino. By the 1920s and for the following few decades, Nesselrode coupes, in which the iced pudding was served not from a larger mold but in individual coupe dishes, were a popular dessert in New York City. It is presumably from this point that the pudding found its home in a pie crust, thanks to Mrs. Hortense Spier.

Hortense Spier was the proprietor of a brownstone restaurant on the Upper West Side. She became something of a pie maven, and the restaurant transformed into a wholesale pie bakery that supplied many of the finest restaurants in the city with a variety of pies, including coconut custard, lemon meringue, and the star of our story, Nesselrode. By 1945, the pies were ubiquitous enough to have captured the attention of the New York Times. A small feature with the title "A Pie Named after a Russian Diplomat" heralded that Nesselrode "recently has begun to appear in a pie." It included a recipe that partially conforms to the classic character of Nesselrode, in that it is a spiked custard lightened with meringue; however, the recipe is more akin to Emma Darwin's than Monni's, as it includes almonds and "macaroons." Like many midcentury desserts, the recipe included gelatin, which would help to maintain its fluffy texture in a refrigerated, but not frozen, form. The pie was topped with bright red maraschino cherries (unrelated to the maraschino liqueur used in early

Nesselrode puddings). Sadly, I have yet to unearth Hortense Spier's actual recipe, or confirm whether the recipe published in the *Times* was meant to replicate hers. Thus, whether she used chestnuts or almonds remains a mystery I may never solve.

As demand grew for Nesselrode pie, Hortense Spier was no longer its sole purveyor, and it naturally evolved. By the 1960s, many published recipes for Nesselrode pie—for instance, in Jell-O and Knox gelatin ads—included no chestnuts at all. It had essentially become a creamy rum-flavored chiffon pie, topped with maraschino cherries, whipped cream, and chocolate shavings. While it was occasionally featured on menus elsewhere, it remained extremely localized to New York City and became a staple at sweet shops and diners. Its prevalence endured through the mid-1960s, and many of the customers who contacted me in hopes of a Nesselrode revival seemed to have this version imprinted in their memories. But then, after enjoying more than twenty years as New York City's favorite pie, for reasons unknown, it swiftly faded into oblivion.

It was important to honor both the true origins of the dessert and the recollections of native New Yorkers in creating my own Nesselrode pie. This turned out to be a protracted undertaking, involving balancing my culinary instincts with the feedback of those who enjoyed the pie so long ago. I was worried that no matter how good it

was, it would never be able to match the potency of flavors that existed only as fond memories.

My first version used gelatin-fortified crème anglaise with chestnut puree. Meringue was folded in, along with candied citrus and cherries macerated in rum. While the Nesselrode nostalgists seemed to appreciate my attempt, it missed the mark. The custard was different from what they remembered, and the candied citrus didn't fit with their idea of the pie. With each subsequent version, I inched away from the profile of the classic Nesselrode pudding and toward the easy, pleasing midcentury-style pie.

One element I would not compromise on, though, was the chestnuts. My final version is a chestnut and rum crème anglaise with gelatin to help it set, folded with silky Italian meringue, and studded with rum-macerated sour cherries. I top it with whipped cream, more sour cherries, and crosshatched ganache. It's nutty, boozy, and fruity, without going the way of an overbearing fruitcake. It's simple enough to appeal to those seeking the straightforward diner classic of their youth, but with the increasingly rare and singular taste of chestnuts tethering it to its French origins. Perhaps in another sixty years, someone will be remembering the alchemy of these flavors and yearning for one more taste.

NESSELRODE PIES

Makes two 9-inch (23-cm) pies

For the chestnut puree:

½ cup (55 g) shelled, peeled chestnuts

2 tablespoons sugar

1 tablespoon rum

For the filling:

½ cup plus ⅔ cup (235 g) sugar

2 tablespoons gelatin

½ teaspoon salt

6 eggs, separated

1½ cups (360 ml) heavy cream

2½ cups (600 ml) whole milk

3 tablespoons dark rum

1 teaspoon vanilla

For the assembly:

2 bottom crusts, blind-baked (1 recipe
   any crust type; see pages 50 and 60)

½ recipe Macerated Cherries
   (page 228)

½ cup (65 g) chocolate shavings or
   ½ recipe Chocolate Ganache for
   Black-Bottom Pies (page 62)

Vanilla Whipped Cream (page 231)

THIS IS A VERY LABOR-INTENSIVE PIE TO CREATE, SO THE RECIPE IS written to make two—give the second one to a friend! Chiffon pies, in which custards or fruit curds are lightened by folding in beaten egg whites, make some people nervous due to the inclusion of uncooked eggs. Here, we go the extra mile and make an Italian meringue in lieu of using uncooked egg whites. Nesselrode pies are often served with chocolate shavings on top, but a cross-hatched drizzle of chocolate ganache is a really elegant touch.

Make the chestnut puree:

In a food processor, pulse to combine the chestnuts and sugar. With the machine running, add the rum and process for about 2 minutes, or until the puree is no longer grainy, stopping every 30 seconds to scrape down the sides. Alternatively, use a mortar and pestle to grind the chestnuts and sugar together, then add the rum and grind into a smooth puree.

Make the filling:

Place a medium mixing bowl in the freezer.

In a large saucepan, combine ½ cup (100 g) of the sugar, the gelatin, and the salt. Whisk in the egg yolks, followed by the chestnut puree. Gradually whisk in the cream, then whisk in the milk. Cook over medium heat, stirring constantly and scraping the bottom of the pan with a rubber spatula, until the mixture reaches 180°F (82°C) on a candy thermometer. Remove from the heat and immediately pour the mixture into the chilled bowl. Stir in the rum. Refrigerate, stirring every 10 minutes, until chilled and thickened, about 40 minutes.

Once the custard has chilled and thickened, in a saucepan, combine the remaining ⅔ cup (135 g) sugar and 3 tablespoons water. Cook over medium heat, stirring with a rubber spatula until the sugar has dissolved and the syrup starts to bubble. Turn off the heat.

Meanwhile, in the bowl of a stand mixer with the whisk attachment or in a large bowl with a hand-held mixer, beat the egg whites until soft peaks form. With the mixer running, pour the hot sugar syrup in a stream into the foamy egg whites, followed by the vanilla. Stop when the meringue holds medium-stiff peaks but is still silky, not foamy.

Transfer most of the meringue from the mixer into a separate bowl, leaving about one-quarter of the meringue on the whisk attachment or in the bowl. Pour the chestnut custard into the mixer bowl and beat it with the residual meringue until smooth. Remove the bowl from the mixer and gently fold the remaining meringue into the mixture.

Assemble the pies:
Pile a heaping cup of filling into each of the pie shells, using a spatula to spread it around the bottoms. Gently fold about two-thirds of the macerated cherries into the remaining filling and divide it into the two pie shells, making sure to scrape the entire contents from the sides of the bowl into the pie, spreading to the edges of the crust and mounding slightly in the center.

Refrigerate the pies for 4 hours, or until set.

If topping with chocolate shavings, sprinkle the tops of the pies with them, then dollop the surface of each with whipped cream and the remaining cherries.

If topping with ganache, transfer the warm ganache to a pastry bag fitted with a narrow tip and pipe it over the pies in a crisscross pattern. Transfer the whipped cream to another pastry bag fitted with a round tip and pipe the whipped cream around the edge of each pie. Top with the remaining cherries.

To serve, slice with a hot, wet knife to avoid dragging the chiffon. Nesselrode pie is best enjoyed right away, but it will keep for up to 2 days, covered, in the fridge.

PISTACHIO CLOUD PIE

Makes one 9-inch (23-cm) pie

For the custard and pie:

¼ cup (30 g) raw organic pistachios

1 cup (200 g) sugar

1 tablespoon gelatin

¼ teaspoon salt

3 eggs, separated

¾ cup (180 ml) heavy cream

1¼ cups (300 ml) whole milk

1 teaspoon vanilla

½ recipe Chocolate Ganache for Black-Bottom Pies (page 62)

1 bottom crust, blind-baked (½ recipe any crust type—I recommend Butter Pastry Dough, page 38, or Gluten-Free Pastry Dough, page 39; see pages 50 and 60)

For the decoration:

1 cup (240 ml) whipping cream

¼ cup (30 g) confectioners' sugar

¼ teaspoon vanilla

Whole shelled pistachios

THIS RECIPE IS INSPIRED BY THE NESSELRODE AND CHIFFON PIES of yesteryear (see page 132 for more on these classic but forgotten delicacies), and it has a creamy, nutty flavor reminiscent of pistachio ice cream. I originally created this recipe to meet the demand for a green pie on Saint Patrick's Day, without having to resort to using green food dye. I've tested it with several types of pistachios in an effort to get the purest pistachio flavor and brightest color. I found that raw organic pistachios tend to have the most vibrant green color and cleanest flavor.

Make the custard and assemble the pie:

Place a large mixing bowl in the freezer.

In the bowl of a food processor, combine the pistachios and ⅓ cup (65 g) of the sugar. Process until the pistachios are completely broken down and about the same size as the sugar granules. Set aside 1 tablespoon to use to decorate the pie.

In a large saucepan, combine ⅓ cup (65 g) of the sugar, the gelatin, and the salt. Whisk in the egg yolks, followed by the pistachio-sugar mixture. Gradually whisk in the cream, then whisk in the milk. Cook over medium heat, stirring constantly and scraping the bottom of the pan with a rubber spatula, until the mixture reaches 180°F (82°C) on a candy thermometer. Remove from the heat and immediately pour the mixture into the chilled bowl. Refrigerate, stirring every 10 minutes, until chilled and thickened, about 40 minutes.

Once the custard has chilled and thickened, in a saucepan, combine the remaining ⅓ cup (65 g) sugar and 2 tablespoons water. Cook over medium heat and stir until the sugar has dissolved and the syrup starts to bubble. Turn off the heat.

Meanwhile, in the bowl of a stand mixer with the whisk attachment or in a large bowl with a hand-held mixer, beat the egg whites until

Continued

soft peaks form. With the mixer running, pour the hot sugar syrup in a stream into the foamy egg whites, followed by the vanilla. Stop when the meringue holds medium-stiff peaks but is still silky, not foamy.

Transfer most of the meringue from the mixer into a separate bowl, leaving about one-quarter of the meringue on the whisk attachment or in the bowl. Pour the cooled pistachio custard into the mixer bowl and beat it with the residual meringue until smooth. Remove the bowl from the mixer and gently fold the remaining meringue into the mixture.

Meanwhile, prepare the ganache as detailed on page 62. Pour about two-thirds of the ganache into the blind-baked pie shell and spread it all over the bottom of the shell. Reserve the remaining ganache for decorating the pie. Transfer the black-bottom shell to the freezer for 5 minutes, until the chocolate is solid.

Pile the filling into the black-bottom pie shell, making sure to scrape the entire contents from the sides of the bowl into the pie, spreading to the edges of the crust and mounding slightly in the center. Refrigerate the pie for 4 hours, or until set.

Decorate the pie:
If the remaining ganache is no longer fluid, reheat it over low heat until it becomes fluid again. Transfer the ganache to a small pastry bag with a fine tip. Apply the ganache in a crosshatch pattern across the surface of the pie, going in one direction then in the other direction at a 45-degree angle.

In the bowl of a stand mixer with the whisk attachment or in a large bowl with a hand-held mixer, whip the cream, confectioners' sugar, and vanilla until stiff peaks form, then transfer the whipped cream to a pastry bag with a plain circular tip. Pipe dollops of whipped cream around the edge of the pie. Sprinkle with the reserved tablespoon of pistachio sugar, then top the whipped cream dollops with whole pistachios.

Serve immediately, cutting with a hot, wet knife to avoid dragging the chiffon. This pie is best enjoyed right away, but it will keep for up to 2 days, covered, in the fridge.

BERRY DREAM PIE

Makes one 9-inch (23-cm) pie

Your preferred Berry Glaze (see
page 143)

¾ cup (180 g) mascarpone, at room
temperature

¼ cup (60 ml) sweetened condensed
milk (canned or homemade; see
recipe on page 230)

Zest of half a lemon

1 tablespoon lemon juice

1 bottom crust, blind-baked (½ recipe
any crust type—I recommend Butter
Pastry Dough, page 38; see pages 50
and 60)

¼ recipe lemon meringue filling or
lemon-elderflower filling (pages 128
and 116)

2 cups (about 250 g) hulled
strawberries, raspberries, black
raspberries, and/or blackberries

I AM OFTEN ASKED ABOUT MY FAVORITE PIE, AND MY ANSWER
varies based on the season. However, I believe that this is the best pie
that I make. It's a good thing I only make it in the summer, because
it's too easy to eat half of one before realizing what you've done. This
pie can be made with strawberries, raspberries, or blackberries,
depending on what's in season.

Whichever berry glaze you are making, in a small bowl, whisk together the cornstarch, sugar, and salt. In the bowl of a blender or food
processor, combine the berries, lemon juice, and cornstarch mixture.
Blend or process the berries into a puree. Transfer the berry puree to
a medium saucepan and cook over medium heat, stirring constantly
and scraping the bottom and sides of the pan with a rubber spatula to
prevent burning. When the mixture starts to bubble strongly, reduce
the heat to low and stir for 5 to 10 minutes more, until it has thickened
enough to coat a wooden spoon. Remove from the heat and allow to
cool slightly at room temperature.

In a food processor or blender, combine the mascarpone, sweetened
condensed milk, lemon zest and juice, and 2 tablespoons of the warm
berry glaze. Blend until there are no longer any lumps of mascarpone
and the mixture is smooth (with the exception of any seeds from
the berries).

Pile the berry mascarpone into the blind-baked pie shell, making
sure to scrape the entire contents from the sides of the bowl into
the pie, and smooth it out with a rubber spatula, easing the mixture
up the side of the shell, leaving about ½ inch (12 mm) of the crust
exposed on the outer edge.

Spoon dollops of the lemon meringue filling on the surface of the
mascarpone and gently spiral into a thin layer without mixing it into
the marscapone. Decorate the pie with the whole berries.

Continued

Spoon the rest of the still-warm glaze over the entire pie, covering the berries, lemon curd, and most of the mascarpone but leaving the outer edge of the crust exposed.

Transfer the pie to the fridge and chill for at least 4 hours before serving. This pie will keep for up to 3 days, covered, in the fridge.

STRAWBERRY GLAZE

2 tablespoons cornstarch

⅓ cup (65 g) sugar

Pinch of salt

½ pound (225 g) strawberries

3 tablespoons plus 1 teaspoon lemon juice

RASPBERRY GLAZE

1 tablespoon plus 2 teaspoons cornstarch

⅓ cup (65 g) sugar

Pinch of salt

½ pound (225 g) raspberries

2 tablespoons plus 1 teaspoon lemon juice

BLACKBERRY GLAZE

1 tablespoon plus 2 teaspoons cornstarch

½ cup (100 g) sugar

Pinch of salt

½ pound (225 g) blackberries

2 tablespoons lemon juice

CHEESECAKE IS A PIE—*THE* PIE, REALLY

Cheesecake is an ancient food, originally used as fuel for Olympians in Ancient Greece then as a wedding dessert for the affluent. From there it spread across Europe and adapted to various regional cuisines before eventually converging in—where else?—New York.

Even before the advent of New York cheesecake as we know it, the American colonies had a tradition of cheesecake that came directly from the English. In fact, Martha Washington's *Booke of Cookery*, which she inherited upon marrying her first husband, had not one but three cheesecake recipes, as well as a recipe for a crustless cheesecake called Curd Pudding. These cakes were made with cheese curds and were flavored with rosewater and spices. Later, Italians brought with them light and airy ricotta cake. But the New York cheesecake we all know and love is made with cream cheese.

Cream cheese is the wholly American invention of a dairyman from Chester, New York, named William Lawrence. Lawrence, a farmhand who married the farmer's daughter, bought a factory in 1872 and began making a soft, milk-based Neufchâtel-style cheese, a variety that was popular at the time. A luxury grocer suggested that he make the cheese richer with the addition of cream, and Lawrence found great success with this innovation. The well-received cream cheese commanded a higher price thanks to the cream, and it captured the attention of Alvah Reynolds, a New York cheese distributor. Reynolds marketed it under the name Philadelphia, relying on that city's reputation for making the finest cheeses. As demand for cream cheese grew, Reynolds started sourcing from other purveyors as well, but sold them all under the same label. Multiple cream cheese companies cropped up in the wake of Philadelphia's success, but Philadelphia is still the one that is synonymous with cream cheese.

At this point you might be wondering how cheesecake fits in with the Jewish foodways often associated with both New York and cheesecake. Cue Arnold Reuben, a Jewish immigrant from Germany and a restaurateur with a string of establishments in Manhattan—and yes, purportedly was the inventor of the Reuben sandwich. While Lindy's, the iconic Broadway restaurant, is credited for making cheesecake famous, Reuben was its originator: After enjoying a cheese curd pie at a party, he re-created the hostess's recipe, substituting cream cheese for the curds. He served it at his restaurants to great acclaim. Later Leo "Lindy" Lindemann, also a German Jewish immigrant, hired Reuben's pastry cook out from under him, and Lindy's cheesecake became famous.

Without a doubt, there exists a vast array of cheesecake types today—among them those made with cottage cheese, ricotta, or cream cheese; crustless, graham cracker–crusted, or bordered with sponge cake; golden or pale; layered with sweetened sour cream or globs of gooey strawberry. One thing is for sure, though: The version of cheesecake we are all most familiar with, the New York cheesecake, is arguably a

pie. Heck, even a Lindy's postcard shows an image of its cheesecake not with the straight sides of a cake, but baked in a pie pan!

I'm fine with it being called cheesecake—I'm not hung up on the name, and after all, some cheesecakes are indeed quite cake-like. But seeing as New York cheesecake is recognized as a cream cheese custard baked in a crust, it falls firmly in the category of pie. Thus, I gladly take it upon myself to grant cheesecake its rightful status as one of the most important foods in American culinary history: pie.

CHEESECAKE

Makes one 9- to 10-inch (23- to 25-cm) cake (pie)

For the crust:

½ recipe Butter Pastry Dough
(page 38)

¼ cup (50 g) sugar

2 tablespoons unsalted butter, melted

For the filling (all ingredients should be at room temperature):

2¾ cups (635 g) cream cheese, about
three 8-ounce (226-g) packages

⅔ cup (165 ml) sour cream

½ cup (120 ml) buttermilk

3 eggs, separated

2 teaspoons lemon juice

1 cup (200 g) sugar

2 tablespoons plus 2 teaspoons flour

Zest from half an orange

Contents of ⅓ of a vanilla bean

¼ teaspoon cream of tartar

MY CHEESECAKE WAS BORN IN NEW YORK, AND I MAKE IT WITH the best cream cheese in New York (Ben's Cream Cheese—not easy to find, but certainly worth seeking out). It might not be as dense as some more famous New York cheesecakes, but I think most people appreciate its lightness. Thanks to the sour cream, buttermilk, and lemon juice, it's also very tangy. I usually find graham cracker crusts disappointing, so of course I use pie crust crumbs instead. Serve on its own or top slices with Sour Cherry or Wild Blueberry Sauce (page 229).

Make the crust:

Preheat the oven to 375°F (190°C). Roll the butter pastry dough to ¼ inch (6 mm) thick and place it on a cookie pan. Bake for 30 minutes, or until puffed up and light golden in color. Allow it to cool, then crumble the crust into small pieces. Grease the bottom and sides of a 9- to 10-inch (23- to 25-cm) springform pan with butter and line the bottom of the pan with a circle of parchment paper.

In a small bowl, combine the pie crust crumbs, sugar, and melted butter, making sure that the sugar and butter are evenly dispersed.

Dump the crumbs into the pan and spread them over the bottom and onto the sides. Press onto the sides first, then the bottom of the pan, evening out the bottom and sides with the back of a measuring cup (or a cup with straight sides), taking care that there isn't a pile-up in the corners. There's no need to press down very hard with the measuring cup or make a completely smooth surface.

Bake for 20 minutes. Transfer the pan to a cooling rack while preparing the filling. Increase the oven temperature to 400°F (205°C).

Make the filling:

In the bowl of a stand mixer with the paddle attachment or in a large bowl with a hand-held mixer, beat the cream cheese, sour

Continued

cream, buttermilk, egg yolks, and lemon juice until the mixture is completely smooth, scraping the sides of the bowl and the paddle attachment occasionally. It may take around 5 minutes until the mixture is completely lump-free.

In a small bowl, combine the sugar and flour, then add this mixture to the cream cheese mixture with the mixer running on low. Mix just until combined. Scrape all the batter from the paddle attachment into the bowl and set aside.

In a small bowl, combine the orange zest and vanilla, then, using a spatula, spread the mixture onto the inside of the mixer bowl. Gradually incorporate the orange-vanilla mixture into the cream cheese mixture by scooping up batter and scraping it onto the sides of the bowl until fully incorporated.

In a clean, dry mixer bowl or a separate large bowl, use the whisk attachment or a hand-held mixer to beat the egg whites and cream of tartar on high speed until stiff peaks form. Pile the beaten egg whites onto the cream cheese batter and use a rubber spatula to gently fold them into the batter, until there are no lumps of egg white.

Gently pour the batter into the prepared crust, making sure to scrape the entire contents from the sides of the bowl into the crust. Place the springform pan on a baking sheet and place it on the middle rack of the oven. Immediately reduce the heat to 250°F (120°C) and bake for 75 minutes. Do not open the oven when the time is up. Instead, turn the oven off and keep the cheesecake in the warm oven for 1 hour. Gently remove from the oven, transferring to a cooling rack to cool to room temperature. Once cooled to room temperature, transfer to the fridge for 3 hours, or until cooled completely.

Use a knife to gently separate the cheesecake from the sides of the pan, then release the sides. Slide a wide spatula under the cheesecake to separate it from the bottom of the pan and gently peel off the parchment paper before transferring it to a serving platter. Slice the cheesecake with a hot, wet knife to avoid dragging and crumbling the filling. The cheesecake will keep for up to 1 week, covered, in the fridge.

BUTTERSCOTCH CREAM PIE

Makes one 9-inch (23-cm) pie

2 tablespoons cornstarch

2 egg yolks

1 egg

½ cup (120 ml) whole milk

6 tablespoons (80 g) unsalted butter

½ cup (100 g) sugar

1 tablespoon plus 1 teaspoon molasses

½ teaspoon salt

½ cup (120 ml) heavy cream

1 teaspoon vanilla

1 bottom crust, blind-baked (½ recipe any crust type; see pages 50 and 60)

Vanilla Sea Salt Meringue (page 231) or Vanilla Whipped Cream (page 231)

ONE NIGHT IN THE EARLY DAYS OF PETEE'S, I WAS CHATTING with a regular customer who had gone to culinary school. She coyly asked me whether I used real scotch whisky in our Butterscotch Cream Pie, and I told her that I didn't use any liquor at all. She nodded in approval—it was a trick question, and I had passed her test. Butterscotch is a caramel made with butter and brown sugar or a touch of molasses instead of plain white sugar, which gives it a more complex flavor. Whether the etymology can be attributed to scotch as a deviation from the word *scorch* or if it refers to a Scottish origin is unknown. Regardless, the caramelized molasses flavor that is the foundation of this recipe is sure to hit the spot.

In a small bowl, whisk together the cornstarch and egg yolks until smooth. Whisk in the whole egg until well combined. Whisk in the milk in a thin stream.

In a large saucepan, melt the butter over medium heat. Whisk in the sugar, molasses, and salt until the sugar has completely dissolved and the mixture is bubbling.

Remove from the heat and immediately whisk in the cream in a thin stream. The butterscotch will bubble wildly.

Remove ¼ cup (60 ml) of the butterscotch from the saucepan and add it to the egg mixture, whisking constantly. Whisk until smooth.

Add the butterscotch-egg mixture to the saucepan, whisking to combine. Cook over medium-low heat, stirring constantly with a rubber spatula, until thickened. Remove from the heat. Add the vanilla and stir well.

Pour the hot butterscotch pudding into the blind-baked crust, making sure to scrape the entire contents from the sides of the pan into the

Continued

pie. Use the spatula to ease the pudding up the sides of the shell, leaving about ½ inch (12 mm) of the crust exposed on the outer edge.

If topping with meringue:
Pile the meringue on top of the pudding, using the back of a hot, wet spoon or an offset spatula to spread the meringue over the pie for a simple presentation (as pictured), or create a wavy texture with peaks and valleys. Alternatively, transfer the meringue to a pastry bag fitted with a fluted or round tip and pipe it on, starting at the outer edge and working your way to the center.

Set the oven rack so that when the pie is on it, the very top of the pie is 3 to 5 inches (7.5 to 12 cm) from the heating element.

Turn the broiler on high. When the heat is in full effect, place the pie under the broiler and set a timer for 1 minute. Broiler heat varies wildly from oven to oven, so keep a close eye on the pie for the entire time it is under the broiler. Heat until the peaks of the meringue turn golden brown, anywhere from 1 to 3 minutes, depending on your oven.

Transfer the pie to the fridge for 4 hours or until cooled completely. To serve, slice with a hot, wet knife in order to avoid dragging the meringue.

If topping with whipped cream:
Chill the pie in the fridge for 1 hour, or until the surface of the pudding is cool to the touch.

Transfer the whipped cream to a pastry bag with a round tip, and pipe the whipped cream onto the pudding, starting at the outer edge and working your way to the center. Refrigerate for 3 hours before serving.

The pie is best eaten the same day, but it will keep for up to 3 days, covered, in the fridge.

Note: I have a few different ways that I like to style meringue. One is to use the back of a hot, wet spoon to create a wavy texture with peaks and valleys (see page 9, bottom left). Another is to fill a pastry bag fitted with a fluted or round tip and pipe on the meringue in dollops starting at the outer edge and working toward the center (see page 9, right). The pie at the top on page 9 shows my favorite way of piping whipped cream. A third option for meringue is to create a smooth flat top with an offset spatula as shown on the opposite page.

HONEY CHÈVRE PIE

Makes one 9-inch (23-cm) pie

For the filling (all ingredients should be at room temperature) and assembly:

2 cups (230 g) chèvre (fresh soft goat or sheep cheese)

⅔ cup (165 ml) honey

½ cup (120 ml) heavy cream

2 eggs

3 egg yolks

¼ teaspoon salt

Zest of half a lemon

Pinch of ground nutmeg

1 bottom crust of Rye Pastry Dough (page 40), crimped and par-baked (½ recipe; see pages 50, 52, and 60)

For the nectarine-thyme topping:

8 ounces (225 g) nectarine slices

¼ cup (60 ml) honey

Juice of 1 lemon

½ teaspoon fresh thyme leaves

Pinch of salt

THE INTRIGUING COMBINATION OF HONEY AND PUNGENT GOAT cheese featured in the Greek and Roman proto-pies inspired this recipe. Since some historians insist that the pies were enveloped in a rye dough, the rye crust is the perfect fit for this recipe. The savoriness of chèvre is complemented by an herbal fruit topping.

Make the filling and assemble the pie:
Preheat the oven to 350°F (175°C).

In the bowl of a stand mixer with the paddle attachment or in a large bowl with a hand-held mixer, beat the chèvre, honey, heavy cream, eggs, egg yolks, salt, lemon zest, and nutmeg until the filling is completely smooth.

Pour the filling into the par-baked crust, making sure to scrape the entire contents from the sides of the bowl into the pie. Bake for 40 minutes, until the center is golden and puffed up.

Transfer the pie to a cooling rack and allow to cool to room temperature, then chill in the fridge for at least 2 hours before serving.

Make the nectarine-thyme topping:
In a large bowl, combine the nectarines, honey, lemon juice, thyme, and salt and allow the topping to macerate at room temperature, covered, for at least 15 minutes.

Slice the pie with a hot knife and serve with the nectarine-thyme topping. The pie will keep for up to 4 days, covered, in the fridge. The topping can be kept in an airtight container for up to 3 days in the fridge.

CUSTARD,
CHESS &
NUT PIES

One of the great things about pies is that they can be made any time of year. While the warmer seasons present us with a carousel of thrilling fruits to work with, the colder months offer other opportunities.

The recipes in this section all belong to a family of interrelated pies that include custard, chess, and nut pies. Since they all contain dairy, eggs, and sugar or some kind of sweetener, I see these pies as existing on a spectrum that ranges from rich and creamy to *super* rich and very sweet—all of which are ideal for a decadent winter treat.

One end of the spectrum is a custard pie, whose filling is generally made with milk and/or cream, eggs, and sugar. Toward the middle of the spectrum is a chess pie. Chess pies are similar to custard pies, but a portion of the liquid dairy is swapped out for melted butter, and the sugar content is higher. Often a bit of flour or cornmeal is added—in some of my recipes I use both. (If you are wondering how the chess pie got its name, see page 174.) At the far end of the sweet spectrum are nut pies, which apart from the nuts are made with butter, a great deal of sugar or syrup, and eggs.

While butter and/or dairy is an important component of these recipes, I don't want to exclude those who can't partake in such things. I've included Vegan Pumpkin Pie (page 196) and Vegan Pecan Pie (page 197) for any vegans who also feel that a holiday dinner is not complete without these delicious desserts.

RONNYBROOK FARM DAIRY, WHERE THE COWS HAVE NAMES

Sometimes when people try the pies at Petee's, they can't quite put their finger on what makes them so delicious, and (surprise!) I think it often comes down to the quality of the ingredients we use. I use milk, butter, and cream from a local dairy called Ronnybrook Farm Dairy in most of the pies I make because the products are high quality, have traveled fewer miles to get to me, and taste damn good. This is especially important for a straightforward custard pie, where the ingredients are so simple and so few.

Ronnybrook also happens to be widely available around New York—their logo of a cow's silhouette has sort of become short-hand for "good milk." Deep down I can be a bit contrarian, so at first their strong branding and ubiquity made me less curious about the people and places behind the product. Some things seem too good to be true, but upon

investigation I learned that Ronnybrook milk is both very good and very true.

In the summer of 2017, my husband, Robert, my daughter, Eloisa, and I were going to be traveling upstate, and I wanted to visit the farm. I could only find a sales email address on the website, and I wasn't really expecting a response. But then I got a voicemail: "Hi Petra, this is Ronny from Ronnybrook." Ronny from Ronnybrook! I couldn't wait to meet him.

Ronny from Ronnybrook is Ronny Osofsky. His family has raised Holstein cattle for seventy years in Pine Plains, New York. Ironically, Pine Plains is a hilly area full of deciduous trees. Ronny and his brother started Ronnybrook Farm Dairy in 1991. Before that, he was a middle school science teacher, but he's always been farming in one form or another.

After a little trouble finding the farm, we met Ronny outside a little white ranch house. He led us into a warehouse-size building on the other side of the dirt road. We put on our hair nets, and Ronny showed us around the dairy plant. He was overwhelmingly generous, and as we went along he loaded us up with delicious dairy things until our hands were too full to carry more. We saw a machine bottling yogurt, mountains of milk crates with glass jugs full of creamline milk (which isn't homogenized so the cream rises to the top), and freshly churned butter being packed by hand.

Next, we went outside and saw the newest calves and the adolescent cows. One calf, born a few days prior, was being bottle fed. Eloisa was almost two and had been very into drinking milk from a bottle ever since she stopped nursing. She stared hard at the bottle-feeding calf, not smiling, completely captivated, and she would've stayed there for a very long time if we didn't have to move along. I think she may have been a little envious, or her mind was blown by the idea that animals could drink from bottles, too. Ronny has about one hundred milking cows and another hundred calves on almost eight hundred acres. That's very few cows per acre compared to most farms, and they all go to pasture on a daily basis. This is almost as unheard of as having a diversified dairy plant where the milk can be processed right on the farm, and Ronnybrook has both. All the cows have names, not numbers. He

showed us the barn where the adult milking cows and a few bulls are kept. He knows which ones like to be pet and which prefer to be left alone. He took us over to pet Sprinkles, a gorgeous Swiss Brown whose handsome tawny color made her stand out among the classic black-and-white Holsteins. After we spent some time admiring her he led us out. "Well, that's it, unless you want to go somewhere scenic."

We all piled into his car. I was expecting to go elsewhere on the farm, but he drove us past several neighboring properties until we reached a gate. He instructed Robert to open it up so we could proceed to the top of a big hill. He pointed out Ronnybrook Farm Dairy in the distance, framed by the Catskills to the west and the Berkshires to the east. He explained that we were on the farm that his parents had bought back in 1946, but aside from that he didn't say too much. I think he wanted the place to speak for itself, as it likely does to him. It was raining and cloudy, but that did nothing to diminish the beauty of the view.

CUSTARD PIES

Makes enough filling for one 9-inch (23-cm) pie

¾ cup (150 g) sugar

Scant ½ teaspoon salt

3 eggs

2 egg yolks

⅔ cup (165 ml) heavy cream

¾ cup (180 ml) evaporated milk (canned or homemade; see recipe on page 230)

2 teaspoons vanilla

Your preferred Custard Filling ingredients (see pages 159–160)

1 bottom crust, crimped and par-baked (½ recipe any crust type; see pages 50, 52, and 60)

CUSTARD PIES OF ALL VARIETIES WERE IMMENSELY POPULAR and ubiquitous on New York City restaurant menus up through the mid-twentieth century. This custard filling is made of the simplest ingredients and has a luscious, flan-like texture. Even better, with this one simple recipe, you can make a number of different custard pies, depending on your fancy.

Preheat the oven to 400°F (205°C).

In a medium bowl, whisk together the sugar, salt, eggs, and egg yolks until smooth. Add the heavy cream in a thin stream, whisking constantly, followed by the evaporated milk and vanilla. Add the additional ingredients called for in your selected filling recipe.

Place the par-baked crust on a baking sheet and pour in the filling, making sure to scrape the entire contents from the sides of the bowl into the pie. Gently cover the crimped crust with a strip of foil or a pie crust protector.

Bake on the lowest rack for 10 minutes, then reduce the temperature to 350°F (175°C) and bake for 35 minutes more, or until the center of the pie has puffed up. Transfer the pie to a cooling rack and allow the pie to cool completely.

Serve the pie at room temperature. It will keep for up to 1 week, covered, in the fridge.

¾ cup (65 g) unsweetened shredded coconut

COCONUT CUSTARD

Of all the custard pies, coconut custard is the most popular in the United States. When we first started selling pies at the Hester Street Fair, before opening our Delancey Street shop, this was one of four core flavors we had on the menu. It was a hit with older customers, who remembered seeing coconut custard pies at restaurants in their youth but hadn't had a good one in years.

Follow instructions on page 158. Spread the shredded coconut on the bottom of the par-baked crust before pouring in the custard filling. The coconut will rise up and float on the surface. Bake until the coconut is golden.

Scant ½ teaspoon freshly grated nutmeg

EGG CUSTARD

Egg custard tarts (which is what the English call pies that have crusts only on the bottom) are a traditional English Christmas dessert. Egg custard pie is remarkably simple—just custard filling with nutmeg baked in a preferred crust—but since it's made with the same essential ingredients as eggnog, it evokes the holidays in a major way.

Follow instructions on page 158. Stir the grated nutmeg into the custard filling before pouring into the par-baked crust.

2 tablespoons orange liqueur, such as Grand Marnier

½ teaspoon freshly grated orange zest

ORANGE CUSTARD

This pie has the flavors of a creamsicle in jiggly pie form—but with a lot more elegance and sophistication.

Follow instructions on page 158. Stir the orange liqueur and zest into the custard filling before pouring into the par-baked crust.

½ cup (100 g) sugar

2 tablespoons heavy cream

Pinch of salt

CARAMEL CUSTARD

The filling of this pie has a flavor similar to flan or crème caramel, but the burnt sugar flavor permeates the entire filling rather than keeping to a thin layer.

Follow instructions on page 158. In a medium saucepan, combine 2 tablespoons water and the sugar. Cook over medium heat, stirring constantly to dissolve the sugar, until the syrup is bubbling. Use a spatula to scrape down any sugar from the sides, then boil for a few minutes more, until the sugar turns a dark amber color. Remove from the heat and whisk in the cream and salt—beware, the cream will bubble up right away. Allow to cool, 3 minutes, then whisk in ¼ cup (60 ml) of the custard filling. Whisk in the remaining custard filling.

1 tablespoon rosewater

½ teaspoon ground cardamom

Optional toppings:

Maple Whipped Cream (page 228)

Dried rose petal flakes

Crushed pistachios

CARDAMOM-ROSE CUSTARD

This custard pie is inspired by luscious Indian desserts that combine rich dairy with rosewater and cardamom, such as kulfi and ras malai. Rosewater can be found at South Asian grocery stores as well as in the specialty sections of larger grocery stores. Dried rose petals can sometimes be found in the bulk tea and spice aisle of health food stores, or from online retailers.

Follow instructions on page 158. Stir the rosewater and cardamom into the custard filling before pouring into the par-baked crust. Serve each slice with a dollop of maple whipped cream, ½ teaspoon rose petals, and/or 1 tablespoon crushed pistachios, if using.

PERSIMMON PUDDING PIE

Makes one 9-inch (23-cm) pie

1 pound (455 g) persimmons or 1¼ cups (300 ml) ready-made persimmon pulp

¾ cup (165 g) packed light brown sugar

½ teaspoon salt

¼ teaspoon ground cinnamon

¼ teaspoon ground allspice

¼ teaspoon ground nutmeg

3 eggs

¾ cup (180 ml) heavy cream

1 teaspoon vanilla

1 bottom crust, crimped and par-baked (½ recipe any crust type; see pages 50, 52, and 60)

PERSIMMON PUDDING ORIGINATED IN THE COLONIAL ERA. Riffing on English favorites like figgy pudding and quince pudding, colonists used the local wild fruit they had available to them—persimmons (*Diospyros virginiana*). Persimmon pie with similar flavors and textures to colonial pudding can be found in pockets of the Midwest, particularly Indiana. It reminds me a little of pumpkin or sweet potato pie, but its flavor is unique and unexpected as well. If you live in an area where you can forage for wild persimmons, I highly recommend using those, but this recipe also works with the Asian persimmons you can find at the grocery store. This pie tastes great with a dollop of Maple Whipped Cream (page 228), the Holiday Custard Sauce (see page 227), or Vanilla Sea Salt Meringue (page 231).

Preheat the oven to 400°F (205°C).

If making your own persimmon pulp, remove the stems from the persimmons along with any seeds (found in wild persimmons). Puree the persimmon flesh in a food processor until smooth. Measure 1¼ cups (300 ml) to use in the pie, and set aside any extra for future use.

In a large bowl, whisk together the brown sugar, salt, cinnamon, allspice, and nutmeg. Whisk in the eggs, then half of the persimmon pulp and half of the heavy cream. Whisk until smooth. Whisk in the remaining persimmon pulp and cream, plus the vanilla, until smooth.

Place the par-baked crust on a baking sheet and pour in the filling, making sure to scrape the entire contents from the sides of the bowl into the pie. Gently cover the crimped crust with a strip of foil or a pie crust protector.

Bake on the lowest rack for 10 minutes, then reduce the heat to 350°F (175°C) and bake for 35 minutes more, or until the surface turns deep orange-brown, similar to pumpkin pie, and the center of the pie has puffed up.

Transfer the pie to a cooling rack and allow the pie to cool for 30 minutes before serving. Serve warm or at room temperature. It will keep for up to 4 days, covered, in the fridge.

SWEET POTATO PIE

Makes one 9-inch (23-cm) pie

2 medium sweet potatoes

⅔ cup (145 g) packed light brown sugar

¼ teaspoon ground nutmeg

¼ teaspoon ground ginger

¼ teaspoon salt

3 eggs

¾ cup (180 ml) evaporated milk (canned or homemade; see recipe on page 230)

½ cup (120 ml) heavy cream

1 teaspoon vanilla

1 bottom crust, crimped and par-baked (½ recipe any crust type; see pages 50, 52, and 60)

PUMPKIN PIE GETS THE TOP BILLING AT THANKSGIVING, BUT I have a soft spot for sweet potato pie. Some people expect it to have a starchy texture, but the secret to making a really good one is to roast sweet potatoes with their skins on—protecting the flesh from drying out in the high heat—until the starches have broken down and deeply caramelized. The end result is a deeply satisfying custard pie with a molasses-y tang.

Preheat the oven to 400°F (205°C).

Prick the sweet potatoes all over with a knife, wrap them in foil, and roast for at least 1 hour, or until you can easily poke a hole in them with the handle of a wooden spoon. Remove from the oven and allow to cool, then remove the flesh from the skins and mash the flesh. Measure 1¼ cups (300 ml) to use for this recipe; save the rest for another purpose (I like to eat it with butter, sea salt, and a pinch of allspice and black pepper).

In a large bowl, whisk together the brown sugar, nutmeg, ginger, and salt. Whisk in the eggs and mashed sweet potato. Gradually whisk in the evaporated milk, cream, and vanilla.

Place the par-baked crust on a baking sheet and pour in the filling, making sure to scrape the entire contents from the sides of the bowl into the pie. Gently cover the crimped crust with a strip of foil or a pie crust protector.

Bake on the lowest rack for 10 minutes, then reduce the heat to 350°F (175°C) and bake for 35 minutes more, or until the surface has turned a warm brown color and the center of the pie has puffed up.

Transfer the pie to a cooling rack and allow the pie to cool for at least 30 minutes before serving. Serve the pie warm or at room temperature. It will keep for up to 5 days, covered, in the fridge.

CLASSIC AMERICAN PUMPKIN PIE IS ACTUALLY FRENCH AND ISN'T MADE OF PUMPKINS

One of the questions that autopopulates on Google when you look up "pumpkin pie" is "how do you make pumpkin pie from a pumpkin?" This indicates that people are ready to resist the reductive simplicity of the canned pumpkin recipe in favor of something a little messier, much fresher, and more in tune with the seasons.

Libby's is easily the most recognizable canned pumpkin purveyor. The company was primarily known for canned meat and dairy until it bought the rights to the Dickinson pumpkin varietal and made canned pumpkin commercially available in 1929.* From that point on, the recipe on the back of the can, which involved both canned pumpkin and canned milk, dominated American kitchens. This is understandable; the reliably smooth and concentrated texture of canned pumpkin is very forgiving and expedient for the home cook. With the commercial availability of canned pumpkin, a baker could whip up a pumpkin pie without having to dissect and disembowel a stubborn old gourd, roast it (but not so aggressively as to dry it out) or steam it and strain the excess liquid, and then puree it into submission.

Pumpkin pie was considered a symbol of American cookery and a Thanksgiving staple since long before the advent of canned pumpkin, however. The legend of the first Thanksgiving brings to mind images of roasted turkeys and pumpkin pies shared by Native Americans and Pilgrims, but of course we know that it didn't really play out that way. Still, pumpkin pie represents a beautiful marriage of indigenous agricultural expertise and European culinary traditions.

By the time the English washed up on American shores, indigenous people had been cultivating gourds for thousands of years. They used the nutritious seeds and even the leaves for sustenance and dried the flesh to store for later reconstitution and consumption. The colonists brought their culinary traditions with them, so at some point they incorporated the pumpkins and squash into pies and custards.

However, some of the desserts made by the colonists would be unrecognizable as pumpkin pie today. Some food historians believe that the pumpkin pie prototype that early settlers in Plymouth in the 1620s may have conceived wasn't even a pie at all. A hollowed pumpkin replaced the crust as a cooking vessel, and inside was a simple egg custard spiced with ginger. Because ovens weren't yet available in the early days of the settlements, the pumpkin was cooked over hot ashes. Later, a pumpkin pie recipe that appeared in a 1672 English cookbook called for pieces of fried pumpkin with apple slices, raisins, fortified wine, and spices, all baked between two layers of crust. However, the oldest published recipe that most closely resembles what we now know as pumpkin pie (it was an eggless sweet pumpkin custard baked in a pastry crust) is actually . . . French. National origin aside, what interests me the most about that recipe, published in 1651 in François Pierre La Varenne's *Le Vrai Cuisinier François* (*The True French Cook*), is the method of cooking the pumpkin.

In my quest for the perfect pumpkin pie recipe I tried dry-roasting butternut squash and kabocha pumpkins** in the oven and found that they tended to dry out in some spots, leading to more waste than I'm comfortable with. Then I tried roasting along with some water in the pan and found that the squash sucked up extra liquid, so I had to strain the flesh afterward to avoid a watery custard. While I don't mind taking extra time for a superior result, I also aim for efficiency. So it finally occurred to me: Why not cook the squash in the dairy? I gave it a shot using bright red kabochas, some milk, and plenty of rich cream. When cooked in the cream and milk, the skin of the squash softened nicely and could be blended right into the custard, lending a deeper color to the pie. On top of that, I found that when I added spices into the hot pumpkin milk, they bloomed beautifully and the aromatics permeated the pie more completely than when added afterward.

Later, when investigating historical pumpkin pie recipes, I found that while the method of cooking pumpkin with dairy is by no means standard, I certainly wasn't the first to do it. François Pierre La Varenne's book was translated into English in 1653, and his recipe for pumpkin "tourte" is as follows: "Boile it with good milk, pass it through a straining pan very thick, and mix it with sugar, butter, a little salt and if you will, a few stamped almonds; let all be very thin. Put it in your sheet of paste; bake it.

After it is baked, besprinkle it with sugar and serve."

Cooking pumpkin in milk and cream allows you to use every bit of the gourd aside from its stem and seeds—no need to scoop the flesh out of the skin. Sure, it's not as quick as using canned pumpkin, but it tastes incredible and makes great use of the abundance of gourds at your farmers' market.

*To be precise, Libby's has never actually sold canned Cucurbita pepo (pumpkin), but a variety of Cucurbita moschata (squash) that is disingenuously called the Dickinson pumpkin. Dickinson pumpkins and the rest of the squash family, including butternuts, neck pumpkins, and cheese pumpkins, simply taste better than genuine pumpkins—even better than the sugar pumpkins some people use for pies. The flavors we associate with pumpkin should actually be attributed to squash instead. For that reason, when I talk about cooking with orange-fleshed gourds, I tend to use the words pumpkin and squash interchangeably.

**Kabochas are also technically squash, not pumpkins.

PUMPKIN PIE

Makes one 9-inch (23-cm) pie

⅔ cup (135 g) sugar

½ teaspoon salt

½ teaspoon ground cinnamon

½ teaspoon ground nutmeg

¼ teaspoon ground cloves

¼ teaspoon ground allspice

3 cups (345 g) pumpkin or winter squash (red kabocha, honeynut, or butternut), cut into 1- to 2-inch (2.5- to 5-cm) pieces

⅔ cup (165 ml) heavy cream

⅔ cup (165 ml) whole milk

1 teaspoon molasses

2 eggs

2 egg yolks

1 bottom crust, crimped and par-baked (½ recipe any crust type; see pages 50, 52, and 60)

Maple Whipped Cream (optional; page 228)

I THINK THIS COMBINATION OF CINNAMON, NUTMEG, CLOVES, and allspice is warm and autumnal, but feel free to substitute or add ginger or even cardamom. In my experience, it's worthwhile to spend more on fresh, high-quality spices.

Preheat the oven to 400°F (205°C).

In a small bowl, whisk together the sugar, salt, cinnamon, nutmeg, cloves, and allspice, ensuring that the spices are evenly dispersed.

In a small saucepan, combine the pumpkin, cream, and milk. Cover with a lid and cook over medium-low heat until the liquid begins to bubble, then remove the lid, reduce the heat to low, and cook until the pumpkin is tender enough to be mashed easily with a fork, about 20 to 30 minutes, stirring every 5 minutes and scraping the bottom of the pot with a rubber spatula to prevent burning.

Stir in the sugar mixture and the molasses and cook for 1 to 2 minutes more, allowing the spices to become fragrant. Transfer the mixture to a blender or food processor or use an immersion blender and puree it until smooth. Allow the mixture to cool for 15 minutes.

Meanwhile, in a small bowl, whisk together the eggs and egg yolks. When the pumpkin puree has cooled slightly, spoon a couple of tablespoons of the puree into the eggs and stir to combine. Pour the egg mixture into the rest of the puree and blend to combine.

Place the par-baked crust on a baking sheet and pour in the filling, making sure to scrape the entire contents from the sides of the bowl into the pie. Bake for 10 minutes, then reduce the heat to 350°F (175°C) and bake for 40 minutes more, or until the center of the pie has puffed up.

Transfer the pie to a cooling rack and allow the pie to cool for at least 30 minutes before serving. Serve the pie warm (my preference) or at room temperature with a generous dollop of maple whipped cream on each serving. It will keep for up to 5 days, covered, in the fridge.

CAJETA MARLBOROUGH PIE

Makes one 9-inch (23-cm) pie

⅔ cup (165 ml) cajeta (canned or homemade; see recipe on page 226), or you can substitute dulce de leche, if you like

⅔ cup (165 ml) heavy cream

2 eggs

2 egg yolks

⅓ cup (65 g) sugar

2 tablespoons sherry

Zest of half a lemon

¼ teaspoon salt

Pinch of ground nutmeg

10 ounces (285 g) peeled, thinly sliced apples (see Note on page 98)

1 bottom crust, crimped and par-baked (½ recipe any crust type; see pages 50, 52, and 60)

MARLBOROUGH PIE IS AN APPLE CUSTARD PIE THAT ORIGINATED in England but developed the alias Deerfield pie in Massachusetts. The first published recipe appeared in *The Accomplisht Cook* in 1660, written by English-born, Paris-trained chef Robert May. It's an intriguing combination of flavors that isn't similar to any modern dish I've tried—lemon, sherry, creamy custard, and apples—but it works. I once incorporated cajeta, a Mexican caramel made with goat milk, into the custard recipe on a whim, thinking that the complex caramelized flavors would meld well with both the sherry and apples. And it is delicious! While Marlborough pie is normally made with sautéed shredded apples, I think thinly sliced apples arranged in a spiral or concentric circles is a really good look.

Preheat the oven to 400°F (205°C).

In a blender, combine the cajeta, cream, eggs, egg yolks, sugar, sherry, lemon zest, salt, and nutmeg.

Arrange the apples slices in the par-baked crust, either in concentric circles or a spiral. Place the crust on a baking sheet and gently pour the custard over the apples, making sure to scrape the entire contents from the sides of the blender into the pie. The apples may float and move out of place—nudge them back into position.

Bake for 10 minutes, then reduce the heat to 350°F (175°C). Bake for 35 to 40 minutes more, or until the pie has a little jiggle if you shake it but is no longer liquid under the surface.

Transfer the pie to a cooling rack and allow to cool completely. Serve at room temperature, slicing with a very sharp knife to cut cleanly through the apples. The pie is best eaten on the same day, but it will keep for up to 5 days, covered, in the fridge.

THE MYTH AND MYSTERY OF CHESS PIE

I had the good fortune of growing up in a pie shop in Virginia, so I've always known the buttery, delicious pleasure of the classic southern treat that is chess pie. Before boutique pie shops started popping up in New York City, though, chess pies weren't much of a thing around here. Still, that hasn't stopped New Yorkers from appreciating them. From the start, people would walk into Petee's, order a chess pie, then ask what chess pie is. It's such a popular question that one of the first things we teach new employees is how to answer it. They'll usually say something along the lines of: "Chess pie is a southern-style custard pie made with butter, buttermilk, and cornmeal."

Which is true, except for when it's not. Chess pie can be found in big swaths of the South, but also in Appalachia and parts of the Midwest. Chess pie always contains butter, but some people will forgo buttermilk and use evaporated milk or cream instead. Some people see no place for cornmeal in a chess pie, but they might use a little flour. Others may use a mix of both. It all depends on the regional foodways and family traditions that a baker is immersed in.

The origin for the name is just as nebulous and undefined. Some people insist that at some point in history, when asked what kind of pie was being served, a waitress answered, "jes' pie" (*just* with a southern accent, I suppose). Another explanation replaces the waitress with a plantation cook.

Legendary southern cook Phila Hach offhandedly wrote as a footnote to her chess pie recipe in the 1970s: "Chess pie gets its name from chestnut meal, which was used in olden days in place of cornmeal." So confident!

Back in colonial times, which is when many people say chess pie originated, pie chests—

stand-alone cabinets that often had perforated metal panels in the doors for airflow—were a common fixture in a kitchen. Chess pie, with all its butter and sugar, lasts quite a while without refrigeration. It could be kept in a pie chest indefinitely without spoiling, so perhaps chess pie is a mispronunciation of chest pie. I just find myself wondering where the *T* went.

Perhaps it's a mispronunciation of cheese pie? The English and the colonists made cheese pies with cheese curds, sugar, eggs, and flavoring such as rosewater and spices. The colonial chess pie is similar but omits the cheese in favor of butter. Maybe a linguistics professor can explain to me how cheese might have become chess as an English accent evolved into an American one. But maybe that question is irrelevant, considering that cheese pies didn't cease to exist when chess pies originated; they existed concurrently and cheese pies were relatively common until they were supplanted by cream cheese–based cheesecakes. (See page 144 for more on that.)

Suffice it to say, I don't have much faith in any of these explanations, and I don't expect a definitive answer to be revealed at this point. Regardless of where the name came from, the tradition of chess pie is quite admirable. It takes the most modest pantry staples and turns them into something rich, elegant, and sublime. Once upon a time, milk was seasonal just as much as any other farm product. Butter could last through the winter, though, as could buttermilk. So while a custard based on milk and cream wouldn't be an option, one based on butter and buttermilk could be, and whatever spices and flavorings were on hand could create endless varieties. And thus, the parameters that hinder one thing become the definitions of a new creation altogether. From there, the tradition of chess pie is up for grabs, so I encourage you to make it yours.

SALTY CHOCOLATE CHESS PIE

Makes one 9-inch (23-cm) pie

½ cup (1 stick/115 g) unsalted butter

3 ounces (85 g) dark chocolate, chopped

2 tablespoons cocoa powder

1 cup plus 2 tablespoons (250 g total) packed light brown sugar

2 tablespoons extra-fine cornmeal

1 teaspoon sea salt

3 eggs

1 egg yolk

¼ cup (60 ml) buttermilk

¼ cup (60 ml) heavy cream

2 teaspoons vanilla

1 bottom crust, crimped (½ recipe any crust type; see pages 50 and 52)

THERE'S A GOOD CHANCE THAT ANY PETEE'S FAN WHO GETS THEIR hands on this book is going to go straight to this recipe. Year in, year out, no matter the weather, this pie is one of our biggest sellers. It gets a deep chocolate flavor from both cocoa powder and dark chocolate, which is beautifully complemented by the sea salt.

Preheat the oven to 400°F (205°C).

In a small saucepan, heat the butter over medium heat just until it melts, then turn off the heat. Whisk in the chocolate and cocoa until the chocolate is completely melted and the mixture is smooth.

In a large bowl, whisk together the brown sugar, cornmeal, and salt. Whisk in the eggs and egg yolk. Whisk in the buttermilk, cream, and vanilla until smooth. Add the chocolate mixture and whisk until fully incorporated.

Place the crust on a baking sheet and pour in the filling, making sure to scrape the entire contents from the sides of the bowl into the pie. Bake for 10 minutes, then reduce the heat to 350°F (175°C) and rotate the pie. Bake for 45 minutes more, or until the center of the pie has puffed up.

Transfer the pie to a cooling rack and allow the pie to cool for 30 minutes to 1 hour before serving. Serve warm or at room temperature. The pie will keep for 1 week (or even longer) at room temperature—but I doubt it will last that long.

Chocolate Coconut Chess Variation:
As a kid, I loved the chocolate coconut chess at my parents' pie shop, which was sweet enough to hurt your teeth—but so good. Add ⅔ cup (55 g) unsweetened shredded coconut to the Salty Chocolate Chess filling before baking to make a less sweet but still deeply satisfying version of my childhood favorite.

LEMON CHESS PIE

Makes one 9-inch (23-cm) pie

1¼ cups (250 g) sugar

2 tablespoons flour

2 tablespoons extra-fine cornmeal

½ teaspoon salt

Zest of 1 lemon

¼ cup (60 ml) freshly squeezed lemon juice, from about 2 to 3 lemons

½ teaspoon vanilla

⅓ cup (75 ml) buttermilk

3 eggs

1 egg yolk

6 tablespoons (80 g) butter, melted and cooled

1 bottom crust, crimped (½ recipe any crust type; see pages 50 and 52)

SIMULTANEOUSLY TART AND RICH, THIS LEMON CHESS PIE IS amazingly versatile and can be dressed up for a dinner party or served straight at a barbecue, and it works well in any season. It's delicious and elegant served with a dollop of whipped cream and a handful of fresh berries. If you'd like the classic pairing of lemon and poppyseeds shown in the photo, see the variation below.

Preheat the oven to 400°F (205°C).

In a medium bowl, whisk together the sugar, flour, cornmeal, and salt. Whisk in the lemon zest and juice, vanilla, buttermilk, eggs, and egg yolk until smooth. Add the melted butter and whisk until well integrated.

Place the crust on a baking sheet and pour in the filling, making sure to scrape the entire contents from the sides of the bowl into the pie. Bake for 15 minutes, then reduce the heat to 350°F (175°C) and bake for 40 minutes more, or until the center is puffed up and the top of the pie is golden.

Transfer the pie to a cooling rack and allow the pie to cool completely before slicing. Serve at room temperature. The pie will keep for up to 1 week at room temperature.

Lemon Poppyseed Chess Variation:
To make a Lemon Poppyseed Chess Pie, use a poppyseed crust (see the Seeded Crust variation, page 48) and swirl 1 tablespoon poppyseeds into the filling before baking.

ALMOND CHESS PIE

Makes one 9-inch (23-cm) pie

1¼ cups (250 g) sugar

3 tablespoons extra-fine cornmeal

3 tablespoons pastry flour

½ teaspoon salt

1 tablespoon plus 1 teaspoon amaretto

½ teaspoon almond flavoring or almond extract

½ teaspoon vanilla

½ cup (120 ml) buttermilk

3 eggs

1 egg yolk

½ cup (1 stick/115 g) unsalted butter, melted and cooled

1 bottom crust, crimped (½ recipe any crust type, plain or black-bottom; see pages 50, 52, and 62)

¼ cup (25 g) sliced almonds

ANOTHER OF MY CHILDHOOD FAVORITES, THIS ALMOND CHESS pie gets its nutty flavor from three separate sources: amaretto and almond flavoring in the filling, and sliced almonds on top. Almond emulsion is a specialty ingredient that is not commonly available in the grocery store but can be purchased through online retailers. I prefer it because it delivers a very intense and persistent almond flavor, but if you can't find it you can substitute almond extract. This filling can be baked into a plain crust for a simple version or in a black-bottom crust made with chocolate ganache for a decadent and elegant dessert.

Preheat the oven to 400°F (205°C).

In a large bowl, whisk together the sugar, cornmeal, flour, and salt. Whisk in the amaretto, almond emulsion, vanilla, buttermilk, eggs, and egg yolk until smooth. Whisk in the melted butter until smooth.

Place the crust (plain or black-bottom) on a baking sheet and pour in the filling, making sure to scrape the entire contents from the sides of the bowl into the pie. Sprinkle the top of the pie with the sliced almonds. Bake for 20 minutes, then reduce the heat to 350°F (175°C) and continue baking for 40 minutes more, or until the center of the pie has puffed up.

Transfer the pie to a cooling rack and allow to cool for 30 minutes to 1 hour before serving. Serve warm or at room temperature. The pie will keep for up to 1 week at room temperature.

CHESTNUT RUM CHESS PIE

Makes one 9-inch (23-cm) pie

½ cup (1 stick/115 g) unsalted butter

1 recipe chestnut puree (see page 136)

1 cup (200 g) sugar

½ teaspoon salt

⅛ teaspoon ground nutmeg

⅛ teaspoon ground allspice

½ teaspoon vanilla

½ cup (120 ml) buttermilk

3 eggs

1 egg yolk

1 bottom crust, crimped (½ recipe any crust type; see pages 50 and 52)

Vanilla Bean Ice Cream (optional; page 229)

INSPIRED BY PHILA HACH'S CHESS PIE ORIGIN THEORY, IN WHICH she said that the name "chess" comes from older recipes that used chestnut flour, I decided to play around with the idea of a chess filling flavored with chestnuts. Since the chestnut puree makes the flour unnecessary, this one can be made gluten-free if you use a gluten-free crust. With the warming flavors of the rum and spices, this pie is great during the autumn and winter—which is also when fresh chestnuts are available!

Preheat the oven to 400°F (205°C).

In a small saucepan, melt the butter over medium heat. Remove from the heat and whisk in the chestnut puree.

In a large bowl, whisk together the sugar, salt, nutmeg, and allspice. Whisk in the vanilla, buttermilk, eggs, and egg yolk until well combined. Whisk in the chestnut butter until the mixture is smooth and consistent.

Place the crust on a baking sheet and pour in the filling, making sure to scrape the entire contents from the sides of the bowl into the pie. Bake for 20 minutes, then reduce the heat to 350°F (175°C). Bake for 40 minutes more, or until the center of the pie has puffed up.

Transfer the pie to a cooling rack and allow to cool for 30 minutes to 1 hour before serving. Serve warm or at room temperature with a scoop of ice cream, if using. The pie will keep for up to 1 week at room temperature.

SESAME CHESS PIE

Makes one 9-inch (23-cm) pie

1¼ cups (250 g) sugar

3 tablespoons extra-fine cornmeal

3 tablespoons all-purpose flour

½ teaspoon salt

3 eggs

2 egg yolks

¼ cup (60 ml) tahini

⅓ cup (75 ml) buttermilk

½ cup (120 ml) heavy cream

1 teaspoon vanilla

1 bottom crust, crimped (½ recipe any crust type; see pages 50 and 52)

2 tablespoons white sesame seeds

THE QUESTION THAT GENERATED THIS RECIPE WAS PRETTY SIMPLE: What if we replaced the butter in a chess pie with a seed or nut butter? To me, tahini was the most interesting "butter" to try. The resulting recipe is a cult hit, especially in our Manhattan location, where we've given this pie the efficient nickname "Chessame."

Preheat the oven to 400°F (205°C).

In a large bowl, whisk together the sugar, cornmeal, flour, and salt. Whisk in the eggs, egg yolks, and tahini until the texture is consistent. Whisk in the buttermilk, cream, and vanilla until smooth.

Place the crust on a baking sheet and pour in the filling, making sure to scrape the entire contents from the sides of the bowl into the pie. Sprinkle the sesame seeds all over the filling. Bake for 20 minutes, then reduce the heat to 350°F (175°C). Bake for 40 minutes more, or until the center of the pie has puffed up.

Transfer the pie to a cooling rack and allow to cool for 30 minutes to 1 hour before serving. Serve warm or at room temperature. The pie will keep for up to 4 days at room temperature.

MEYER LEMON SUNSHINE PIE

Makes one 9-inch (23-cm) pie

2 Meyer lemons

3 eggs

2 egg yolks

1½ cups (300 g) sugar

¼ teaspoon salt

3 tablespoons cream cheese

⅓ cup (75 ml) sour cream

5 tablespoons (70 g) unsalted butter, melted

1 bottom crust, crimped (½ recipe any crust type; see pages 50 and 52)

THIS PIE IS SIMILAR TO A CHESS PIE IN THAT IT'S MADE WITH A good deal of butter, dairy, and sugar. However, the final result has a much more potent punch of lemon than a lemon chess pie. Why? Because whole Meyer lemons—peel and all—are pulverized into the filling. The result is simultaneously buttery, tangy, sweet, and zesty. Don't attempt to substitute the Meyer lemons with regular lemons, because the result would be overwhelmingly bitter. I like to balance the tartness of this pie with a scoop of Vanilla Bean Ice Cream (page 229).

Preheat the oven to 400°F (205°C).

Slice the lemons into wedges and remove any visible seeds. In a food processor or blender, combine the lemon wedges, eggs, egg yolks, sugar, salt, cream cheese, and sour cream. Process on high speed until the ingredients are fully combined. Add the melted butter and blend until smooth, pausing every so often to scrape down the sides with a rubber spatula.

Place the crust on a baking sheet and pour in the filling, making sure to scrape the entire contents from the sides of the bowl into the pie. Place in the oven and immediately reduce the heat to 350°F (175°C). Bake for 50 to 55 minutes, or until the top is a warm golden color and the center has puffed up.

Transfer the pie to a cooling rack and allow to cool completely before slicing. Serve at room temperature. The pie will keep for up to 5 days at room temperature.

CAJETA MACADAMIA PIE

Makes one 9-inch (23-cm) pie

1 cup (240 ml) cajeta (canned or home-made; see recipe on page 226)

⅔ cup (145 g) packed light brown sugar

3 eggs

1 egg yolk

½ teaspoon vanilla

½ cup (1 stick/115 g) unsalted butter, melted

1 cup (135 g) roasted salted macadamia nuts

1 bottom crust, crimped (½ recipe any crust type; see pages 50 and 52)

THIS PIE IS UNIQUE IN TASTE AND TEXTURE—A COMPLEX CAJETA (Mexican goat milk caramel with a hint of cinnamon) is a perfect partner for buttery roasted macadamias. Because of the addition of butter, technically the filling falls somewhere between a custard and a chess pie.

Preheat the oven to 400°F (205°C).

In a blender, combine the cajeta, brown sugar, eggs, egg yolk, and vanilla at a medium speed until smooth. Add the melted butter and blend briefly, until the filling is consistent.

Place the crust on a baking sheet. Place the macadamias in the bottom of the crust, then pour in the filling, making sure to scrape the entire contents from the sides of the blender into the pie—the macadamias will rise up and float on the surface. Bake for 10 minutes, then reduce the heat to 350°F (175°C), and bake for 45 to 50 minutes more, or until it puffs up around the edges.

Transfer the pie to a cooling rack and allow to cool for 45 minutes. Serve warm or at room temperature. The pie will keep for up to 1 week at room temperature.

BROWN BUTTER–HONEY PECAN PIE

Makes one 9-inch (23-cm) pie

½ cup (1 stick/115 g) unsalted butter

1 cup (220 g) packed light brown
    sugar

3 eggs, beaten

1 egg yolk

½ teaspoon salt

1 teaspoon vanilla

½ cup (120 ml) honey

1 bottom crust, crimped (½ recipe any
    crust type; see pages 50 and 52)

1 cup (120 g) pecan halves

MOST PECAN PIES ARE MADE WITH CORN SYRUP, WHICH YOU won't find in my recipes. However, the first pecan pies predated the invention of corn syrup and were actually rich dairy custards—think coconut custard but with pecans. I love the buttery, sticky sweetness of pecan pie, though, so I use brown sugar and local apple blossom honey, taking a few extra minutes to brown the butter, rather than just melting it, for a nuttier, caramelized flavor. The combination of honey and browned butter gives this pecan pie complexity and character.

Preheat the oven to 400°F (205°C).

In a lightly colored medium saucepan (so that you can see the color of the butter as it cooks—white enamel or stainless steel both work well), melt the butter over medium heat. After the butter melts and begins to bubble, heat for 5 to 10 minutes more, stirring with a wooden spoon, until the butter browns. When the butter is sufficiently browned, small chunks of toasty brown caramelized milk solids will have formed, and the rest of the butter will have a deep, golden-brown hue. Allow the browned butter to cool in the pan for 10 minutes.

Meanwhile, in a large bowl, combine the brown sugar, eggs, egg yolk, salt, and vanilla.

Whisk the honey into the warm browned butter. Whisk the honey-butter mixture into the sugar mixture. Use a rubber spatula to scrape every bit of honey butter from the pan and stir until smooth.

Place the crust on a baking sheet. Place the pecans in the bottom of the crust, then pour in the filling, making sure to scrape the entire contents from the sides of the bowl into the pie. Bake for 10 minutes, then reduce the heat to 350°F (175°C) and bake for 45 minutes more, or until the center of the pie has puffed up.

Transfer the pie to a cooling rack and allow to cool for 30 minutes before serving. Serve warm or at room temperature. The pie will keep for up to 1 week at room temperature.

MAPLE-WHISKEY WALNUT PIE

Makes one 9-inch (23-cm) pie

½ cup (1 stick/115 g) unsalted butter

1 cup (220 g) packed light brown
    sugar

3 eggs, beaten

1 egg yolk

½ teaspoon salt

2 tablespoons bourbon whiskey

1 cup (125 g) walnut halves (see Note)

½ cup (120 ml) maple syrup

1 bottom crust, crimped (½ recipe any
    crust type; see pages 50 and 52)

Note: If you are lucky enough to find to
black walnuts, as opposed to the ubiquitous English walnuts, use them in
this pie! English walnuts actually originated in Persia and are less expensive,
because they have large, mildly flavored nutmeats that are easier to shell.
Black walnuts are native to North
America and much more laborious to
process, but their flavor is unique and
indescribable—vastly more interesting
than their Old World cousins.

THIS IS A VARIATION ON PECAN PIE THAT USES MAPLE SYRUP AS A sweetener and gets a little kick from bourbon. Use only 100 percent real maple syrup and choose one with a dark, robust flavor. (It used to be labeled "grade B," but this confusing classification has changed. Dark maple syrup has simply been further caramelized, so it has a more intense flavor than the light amber syrup.) As with the Brown Butter–Honey Pecan Pie (page 190), using browned butter deepens the flavor of the filling.

Preheat the oven to 400°F (205°C).

In a lightly colored medium saucepan (so that you can see the color of the butter as it cooks—white enamel or stainless steel both work well), melt the butter over medium heat. After the butter melts and begins to bubble, heat for 5 to 10 minutes more, stirring with a wooden spoon, until the butter browns. When the butter is sufficiently browned, small chunks of toasty brown caramelized milk solids will have formed, and the rest of the butter will have a deep, golden-brown hue. Allow the browned butter to cool in the pan for 10 minutes.

Meanwhile, in a large bowl, combine the brown sugar, eggs, egg yolk, salt, and whiskey.

Whisk the maple syrup into the warm browned butter. Whisk the maple-butter mixture into the sugar mixture. Use a rubber spatula to scrape every bit of maple butter from the pan and stir until smooth.

Place the crust on a baking sheet. Place the walnuts in the bottom of the crust, then pour in the filling, making sure to scrape the entire contents from the sides of the bowl into the pie. Bake for 10 minutes, then reduce the heat to 350°F (175°C) and bake for 45 minutes more, or until the center of the pie has puffed up.

Transfer the pie to a cooling rack and allow to cool for 30 minutes before serving. Serve warm or at room temperature. The pie will keep for up to 1 week at room temperature.

PONY PIE

Makes one 9-inch (23-cm) pie

½ cup (1 stick/115 g) unsalted butter

½ cup (120 ml) honey

1 cup (220 g) packed light brown sugar

3 eggs

½ teaspoon salt

2 tablespoons bourbon whiskey

½ cup (50 g) whole walnuts

½ cup (50 g) whole pecans

½ cup (85 g) chopped dark chocolate

1 bottom crust, crimped (½ recipe any crust type; see pages 50 and 52)

MANY BUSINESSES, INCLUDING MY PARENTS', HAVE ENDEAVORED to make a chocolate-nut pie and then made the mistake of calling it Derby Pie. The thing is, Derby Pie is not merely a type of pie; it is a registered trademark of a product first made by the Kern family at the Melrose Inn in Prospect, Kentucky. So if you dare to call your pie that, be prepared for a cease-and-desist letter at the very least! Still, around Kentucky Derby time, I tend to receive requests for a chocolate nut pie, so what's a baker to do? Try making this Pony Pie, which is sort of a mash-up of my walnut and pecan recipes, with the addition of chopped dark chocolate. Feel free to make it for any occasion, not just a horse race.

Preheat the oven to 400°F (205°C).

In a small saucepan, melt the butter over medium heat. Remove from the heat and allow to cool for 10 minutes, then whisk the honey into the melted butter. Set aside.

In a large bowl, whisk together the brown sugar, eggs, salt, and bourbon. Whisk the honey butter into the sugar mixture until smooth. Stir in the walnuts, pecans, and chocolate.

Place the crust on a baking sheet. Pour in the filling, making sure to scrape the entire contents from the sides of the bowl into the pie. Place on the middle rack of the oven and bake for 10 minutes, then reduce the heat to 350°F (175°C) and bake for 40 minutes more, or until the center of the pie has puffed up.

Transfer the pie to a cooling rack and allow to cool for 30 minutes before serving. Serve warm or at room temperature. The pie will keep for up to 1 week at room temperature.

VEGAN PUMPKIN PIE

Makes one 9-inch (23-cm) pie

1 pound (455 g) pumpkin or winter squash (red kabocha, honeynut, or butternut), cut into 1-inch (2.5-cm) chunks

½ teaspoon salt

½ teaspoon ground cinnamon

½ teaspoon ground nutmeg

¼ teaspoon ground cloves

¼ teaspoon ground allspice

½ cup (45 g) rolled oats

¼ cup (35 g) chestnut flour

3 tablespoons tapioca starch

⅔ cup (145 g) light brown or unrefined sugar

3 tablespoons refined coconut oil

1 bottom crust of Vegan Pastry Dough (page 39), crimped and par-baked (½ recipe; see pages 50, 52, and 60)

MY HEART GOES OUT TO THE VEGANS ON THANKSGIVING. It's easy to make satisfying and hearty vegan dishes for Thanksgiving dinner, but dessert is another story. I noticed that lots of vegan pumpkin pies substitute coconut milk for dairy. As much as I love coconut, I want my pumpkin pie straight. I developed this recipe to make a warmly spiced pumpkin pie that set nicely and was rich— without tasting of coconut. Refined coconut oil adds richness without a strong coconut flavor, chestnut flour adds a subtle nuttiness and depth, and tapioca starch aids in setting.

Preheat the oven to 425°F (220°C).

In a medium saucepan, combine 1½ cups (360 ml) water with the pumpkin, salt, cinnamon, nutmeg, cloves, and allspice. Bring the water to a boil over high heat, then cover with a lid and reduce the heat to low. Simmer, stirring occasionally, until the pumpkin is tender but not broken down, about 15 minutes. Stir in the oats and cook just until oats are cooked through, about 5 minutes more. Transfer the pumpkin mixture to a blender or food processor, or leave in the pan if using an immersion blender.

Meanwhile, in a small bowl, whisk together the chestnut flour, tapioca starch, and brown sugar. Stir the sugar mixture and coconut oil into the pumpkin mixture and blend everything together until fully incorporated.

Place the par-baked crust on a baking sheet and pour in the filling, making sure to scrape the entire contents from the sides of the bowl into the pie. Bake for 10 minutes, then reduce the heat to 350°F (175°C) and bake for 50 minutes more, or until the surface is a deep warm brown and it jiggles slightly when gently shaken.

Allow the pie to cool completely before slicing. Serve at room temperature. Keep covered in the fridge for up to 5 days.

VEGAN PECAN PIE

Makes one 9-inch (23-cm) pie

¾ cup (165 g) packed light brown sugar

¼ cup (120 g) tapioca flour

¾ teaspoon salt

½ cup (120 ml) coconut oil, melted over low heat, if needed

¾ cup (180 ml) maple syrup

½ cup (120 ml) almond milk

2 teaspoon vanilla

1 bottom crust of Vegan Pastry Dough (page 39), crimped (½ recipe; see pages 50 and 52)

1 cup (120 g) pecan halves

WHEN CREATING VEGAN RECIPES, IT'S HELPFUL TO BE FLEXIBLE and think outside the box. My regular pecan pie has the distinct flavor of brown butter and honey, both of which are nonvegan ingredients, so I don't try to replicate it. Instead, this vegan pecan pie uses coconut oil and maple syrup while tapioca flour takes on the role of thickener, replacing eggs. A bit of almond milk and plenty of pecans imbue the pie with nuttiness. Does it taste like my regular pecan pie? Nope. Does it satisfy a vegan's craving for the brown sugary crunch of pecan pie? It sure does!

Preheat the oven to 400°F (205°C).

In a large bowl, combine the sugar, flour, and salt. Mix thoroughly with a whisk so that the starch is evenly dispersed, then whisk in the coconut oil. Add the maple syrup and whisk thoroughly, followed by the almond milk and vanilla.

Place the pie dish with bottom crust on a baking sheet. Pour in the filling, making sure to scrape the entire contents from the sides of the bowl into the pie. Sprinkle the pecans over the top, or arrange the nuts in concentric circles if you'd like an especially elegant presentation. Bake the pie for 10 minutes, then reduce the heat to 350°F (175°C) and bake for 40 minutes more.

Transfer the pie to a cooling rack and allow to cool to room temperature before serving. The pie will keep for up to 1 week at room temperature.

SAVORY PIES
&
QUICHES

When we opened our shop in 2014, Petee's swiftly became famous for our sweet pies, and since we stay open until midnight (and later on the weekends), we developed a reputation as a great late-night dessert stop. We also put a few savory pies on the menu, too, and while they stayed out of the limelight, they developed a small cult following. That's why when we opened the café a few years later, I was excited about the opportunity to expand the menu by adding more delicious savory pies. After all, the café is a larger space than a shop, allowing people to visit throughout the day and linger over coffee, sip natural wine, and have both dinner *and* dessert.

One thing that I love about making savory pies is that it's yet another way we can support and deepen our relationship with the farmers who grow our food. We use seasonal vegetables and herbs along with responsibly raised meat from local farms to make ever-evolving versions of our luscious Quiche (page 216) and homey Chicken Pot Pies (page 220). Customers enjoy these savory pies with a simple side salad to make a complete meal. They're on the menu year-round, but they never get boring because their components change with the seasons, from ramps and fiddleheads in the springtime to kale and butternut squash in the winter.

Some of the recipes in this section are quick and easy, like the quiche and the Tomato Ricotta Pie (page 200). Others require more time and effort, like the Meat and Potato Pie (page 208) and the Chicken Pot Pies. Some come from the English tradition of savory pies, like the Cheshire Pork Pie (page 210), and others, like the Chile Verde Pork Pie (page 204), are new inventions that reimagine familiar flavors in the form of a pie. All of them are made for a crowd and will give you the satisfaction of a wholesome meal.

TOMATO RICOTTA PIE

Makes one 9-inch (23-cm) pie

2 cups (490 g) ricotta cheese

1 egg

1 egg yolk

1 cup (100 g) grated hard cheese (Parmesan, Pecorino, or Gruyère)

2 tablespoons minced basil

1 tablespoon minced oregano

1 tablespoon minced garlic

1 teaspoon salt

¼ teaspoon freshly ground black pepper

1 bottom crust of Rye Pastry Dough (page 40), crimped (½ recipe; see pages 50 and 52)

1 pound (455 g) heirloom tomatoes in various colors, cut in ¼-inch (6-mm) slices

Toasted pine nuts, for garnish

Sea salt, for garnish

Olive oil, for garnish

THIS PIE COMES TOGETHER QUICKLY AND EASILY AND IS PERFECT with a side salad for a casual summer brunch. Like any pie, its flavor is completely dependent on the quality of produce you use, so seek out the most vibrant and flavorful tomatoes you can find! Lackluster grocery store tomatoes need not apply. It's especially pretty when you use more than one color of tomato on top—have fun layering purple, yellow, and deep red slices. A rye or whole wheat crust makes this pie especially wholesome, but it works beautifully with a gluten-free or butter crust as well.

Preheat the oven to 400°F (205°C).

In a large bowl, whisk the ricotta, egg, and egg yolk until smooth. Stir in the cheese, basil, oregano, garlic, salt, and pepper until the herbs are well distributed.

Place the crust on a baking sheet and pour in the filling, making sure to scrape the entire contents from the sides of the bowl into the pie. Smooth the top, then layer the tomato slices so that they overlap, alternating colors. The extent to which they overlap depends on the size of the tomato slices.

Bake for 20 minutes, then reduce the heat to 350°F (175°C) and bake for 25 minutes more. The filling will puff up slightly.

Transfer the pie to a cooling rack and allow to cool for 20 minutes. Serve warm, cutting with a very sharp knife to slice cleanly through the tomatoes. Sprinkle each slice with toasted pine nuts, sea salt, and/or a drizzle of olive oil. The pie will keep for up to 3 days, covered, in the fridge.

CHEESE AND ONION PIE

Makes one 9-inch (23-cm) pie

2 tablespoons unsalted butter

2 onions, quartered and finely sliced

1 teaspoon salt

½ teaspoon freshly ground black pepper

1 Yukon gold potato, coarsely grated

¼ cup (60 ml) heavy cream

¼ cup (60 ml) whole milk

6 ounces (170 g) grated hard cheese or crumbled soft cheese, about 1½ cups

2 tablespoons minced chives

1 recipe Butter Pastry Dough (page 38), bottom crust prepared to make a double-crust pie (see pages 50 and 53)

Egg Wash (page 56)

Sprig of thyme

CHEESE AND ONION PIE IS AN ENGLISH CLASSIC THAT IS TYPICALLY made with Red Leicester cheese or aged cheddar. I like to make this pie with a bright orange Mimolette-style cheese called Harvest Moon, made in Goshen, New York, which lends not only its beautiful color but a nutty flavor as well. Alternatively, using an aged cheddar like Cabot cloth-bound makes for a rich and intense filling, while a soft farmer's cheese makes a lighter and milder pie. Use red or yellow onions for a bold onion flavor, or for a milder flavor use sweet or white onions.

Preheat the oven to 400°F (205°C).

In a large saucepan, melt the butter over medium heat. Add the onions, salt, and pepper and sauté, stirring frequently, until soft, about 4 to 5 minutes. Add the potato and cook for 1 minute more. Remove from the heat and stir in the cream and milk, followed by the cheese and chives. Pour the filling into the bottom crust, making sure to scrape the entire contents from the sides of the pan into the pie.

Top the pie with the top crust according to the instructions on page 53. Brush the top crust with the egg wash, then gently press the sprig of thyme onto the egg-washed crust. Place the pie on a baking sheet to collect any juices that bubble over. Bake for 15 minutes, then reduce the heat to 350°F (175°C) and bake for 40 minutes more, or until the filling has been bubbling for at least 10 minutes.

Transfer the pie to a cooling rack and allow to cool for at least 20 minutes before serving. Serve warm. The pie will ooze delicious melted cheese, but that only adds to its appeal! The pie will keep for up to 4 days, covered, in the fridge.

CHILE VERDE PORK PIE

Makes one 9 by 13-inch (23 by 33-cm) pie or 10-inch (25-cm) deep-dish pie

3 pounds (1.4 kg) boneless pork shoulder

2 poblano chiles

2 jalapeños

1 medium white onion, minced

6 cloves garlic, slivered

1 cup (135 g) minced tomatillos

1 cup (100 g) quartered tomatillos

1 tablespoon chopped fresh oregano

2 teaspoons salt

Freshly ground black pepper

½ recipe Corn Pastry Dough (page 39, made by hand using the method on page 42)

2 tablespoons cornstarch

Juice of 1 lime

1 cup (40 g) chopped cilantro

Egg Wash (page 56)

Note: This recipe is too large for a standard pie pan. A 9 by 13-inch (23 by 33-cm) baking dish or casserole dish, or a 10-inch (25-cm) deep-dish pie pan are all good options.

THIS PIE COMBINES ALL THE ELEMENTS OF A GOOD CHILE VERDE—succulent pork shoulder, tangy tomatillos, green chiles, fresh cilantro—and tops it off with a crunchy cornmeal crust.

Preheat the oven to 275°F (135°C).

Separate the fat from the meat of the pork shoulder. Cut the fat into ¼-inch (6-mm) pieces and cut the meat into ½-inch (12-mm) pieces, and place both in your baking dish (see Note).

If you'd like to keep a moderate spice level, remove the stem, seeds, and ribs of the poblano and jalapeño chiles before cutting them into ¼-inch (6-mm) pieces. Take care when handling the chiles—avoid touching your face and wear gloves, if possible. For those with a high spice tolerance, include a portion of the ribs and seeds. Add the diced chiles, the onion, garlic, minced and quartered tomatillos, oregano, salt, and pepper to taste to the pork and toss to combine. Cover the baking dish with a lid or aluminum foil.

Place the dish in the oven and cook for 4 hours, stirring every hour. Remove the pan from the oven and increase the heat to 400°F (205°C).

Roll out the corn pastry dough into a shape that will cover your baking dish, using the method on page 50.

Put the cornstarch in a small bowl. Remove ¼ cup (60 ml) of the liquid from the baking dish and pour it over the cornstarch, whisking it quickly to make a slurry. Mix the slurry, the lime juice, and the cilantro into the dish.

Top the baking dish with the dough. Brush with the egg wash, pierce the crust with a knife to make evenly spaced vents, then bake, uncovered, for approximately 30 minutes, or until the crust is fully cooked and golden brown. Transfer the pie to a cooling rack and allow to sit for 10 to 15 minutes. Serve while still hot. The pie will keep for up to 4 days, covered, in the fridge.

SAVORY MINCEMEAT PIE

Makes one 9-inch (23-cm) pie

4 ounces (115 g) peeled apples, cut into ½-inch (12-mm) cubes

¼ cup (55 g) halved sour cherries

2 ounces or a heaping ⅓ cup (60 g) dried black currants (not Zante currants; see Note on page 80)

2 ounces or a heaping ⅓ cup (60 g) raisins

¼ Meyer lemon, seeds removed, minced with its peel

Scant ½ cup (55 g) raw beef suet, shredded with a grater

2 tablespoons packed dark brown sugar

1 teaspoon salt

½ teaspoon freshly ground black pepper

½ teaspoon ground cinnamon

½ teaspoon ground allspice

¼ teaspoon ground nutmeg

¼ teaspoon ground cardamom

⅛ teaspoon ground cloves

¼ cup (60 ml) brandy or rum

¼ cup (60 ml) port, sweet sherry, or pommeau

4 ounces (115 g) venison or beef, minced or ground

1 recipe Lard Pastry Dough (page 40), bottom crust prepared to make a double-crust pie (see pages 50 and 53)

Egg Wash (page 56)

THE ENGLISH MINCE PIE AND AMERICAN MINCEMEAT PIE DESCEND from the same culinary ancestor, sweet and savory Middle Eastern dishes that combined meat, spices, and fruits. The modern English mince pie no longer includes meat and has become a full-on dessert (see page 105 for my take on this). Many New Englanders, on the other hand, use heirloom recipes that include meat and animal fat (typically suet, which is the raw beef fat that is located near the kidneys). Please note that the filling for this recipe is meant to age for at least 2 weeks, then the meat is added right before baking. I recommend using a lard crust and serving the pie with other savory dishes at a holiday dinner.

In a medium bowl, combine the apples, cherries, currants, raisins, lemon, and suet.

In a small bowl, whisk together the brown sugar, salt, pepper, cinnamon, allspice, nutmeg, cardamom, and cloves. Pour the sugar mixture over the fruit and toss to coat. Transfer the mixture to a large glass jar or a container with an airtight lid, and pour the brandy and port over the mixture. Tighten the lid and allow to age for at least 2 weeks in the fridge.

When you are ready to make the pie, preheat the oven to 400°F (205°C). Pour the contents of the jar into a large bowl. Add the meat and stir to combine. Pour the filling into the bottom crust, making sure to scrape the entire contents from the sides of the bowl into the pie.

Top the pie with the top crust according to the instructions on page 53. Brush the top crust with the egg wash. Place the pie on a baking sheet to collect any juices that bubble over. Bake for 15 minutes, then reduce the heat to 350°F (175°C) and continue to bake for 40 minutes more, or until the filling has been bubbling for at least 10 minutes.

Transfer the pie to a cooling rack and allow to cool for 20 minutes. Serve warm. The pie will keep for up to 4 days, covered, in the fridge.

MEAT AND POTATO PIE

Makes one 9 by 13-inch (23 by 33-cm) pie or 10-inch (25-cm) deep-dish pie

¼ cup (½ stick/55 g) unsalted butter

1 large sweet onion, chopped into
    ½-inch (12-mm) pieces

2 tablespoons minced garlic

½ cup (70 g) finely diced carrot and/
    or parsnip

1 cup (140 g) finely diced Yukon gold
    potato

1 pound (455 g) stew meat (beef,
    venison, goat, or lamb), cut into
    ½-inch (12-mm) cubes

1 tablespoon cornstarch

1 tablespoon salt

½ teaspoon freshly ground black
    pepper

2 stalks celery, diced

2 tablespoons tomato paste

2 tablespoons packed dark brown
    sugar

1 tablespoon chopped fresh rosemary

1 cup (240 ml) red wine

1 cup (240 ml) chicken or beef stock

½ recipe Whole-Wheat Pastry Dough
    (page 40)

Egg Wash (page 56)

THIS PIE IS DEEPLY SATISFYING IN THE COLDER MONTHS, AND YOU can use any red meat you like—lamb, venison, beef, or even goat. This pie is made in a pot-pie style (with the crust only on top), and the whole-wheat crust makes a very hearty and savory topping.

In a large saucepan, melt 3 tablespoons of the butter over medium-high heat. Add the onion, garlic, carrot, and potato and sauté until the onion turns translucent, about 5 minutes. Transfer the vegetables to a bowl and set aside, leaving as much butter as you can in the pan.

In a medium bowl, toss the meat with the cornstarch, salt, and pepper, and add it to the pan with the remaining 1 tablespoon butter. Cook over high heat for 3 to 4 minutes, or until the meat has browned.

Add the celery, tomato paste, brown sugar, and rosemary and stir to combine. Add the sautéed vegetables back to the pan. Pour in the wine and bring to a simmer, using a wooden spoon to scrape up any caramelized bits from the bottom of the pan. Add the stock, return to a simmer, then reduce the heat to low and cover the pot with a tight-fitting lid. Simmer for 1 hour, or until the meat is tender.

Meanwhile, preheat the oven to 350°F (175°C). Roll out the rye pastry dough into a shape that will cover your baking dish, using the method on page 50.

Transfer the filling to your baking dish (see Note on page 204). Top the baking dish with the dough. Brush with the egg wash, pierce the crust with a knife to make evenly spaced vents, then bake for 1 hour, or until the crust is deep golden.

Transfer the pie to a cooling rack and allow to cool for at least 15 minutes before serving. Serve hot. The pie will keep for up to 4 days, covered, in the fridge.

CHESHIRE PORK PIE

Makes one 9-inch (23-cm) pie

1 teaspoon cornstarch

½ teaspoon ground nutmeg

1½ teaspoons salt

¼ teaspoon freshly ground black pepper

1 tablespoon finely minced herbs (such as sage, rosemary, and/or thyme)

8 ounces (225 g) peeled, thinly sliced apples

1 pound (455 g) pork loin, cut into ⅛- to ¼-inch- (3- to 6-mm-) thick slices

1 recipe Butter Pastry Dough (page 38), bottom crust prepared to make a double-crust pie (see pages 50 and 53)

2 tablespoons unsalted butter, cut into four pieces

1 cup (240 ml) white wine (off-dry to medium-sweet)

Egg Wash (page 56)

CHESHIRE PORK PIE, LIKE SO MANY MEAT PIES, HAILS FROM England. Old recipes for this pie are remarkably simple: Layer seasoned chunks of pork loin with apple slices in pastry dough, sprinkle with sugar, and pour a pint of wine over the filling before enclosing it in the crust and baking. This version is still quite simple, but the addition of herbs makes it decidedly more savory. I forgo the sugar and use only a cup of slightly sweet wine instead—an off-dry Riesling is a good option. Use a sturdy, sharp apple—Rhode Island Greening and Ashmead's Kernel are both great if you can find them, but Granny Smith will do the trick as well.

Preheat the oven to 400°F (205°C).

In a medium bowl, whisk together the cornstarch, nutmeg, salt, pepper, and herbs. Add the apples and gently toss to coat.

Arrange about one-third of the pork slices in a thin layer in the bottom crust. Layer half of the apples over the pork. Layer on another third of pork, followed by the rest of the apples. Add the rest of the pork. Dot with the butter, sprinkle with any dry ingredients and herbs that remain in the bowl, and pour the wine over top.

Top the pie with the top crust according to the instructions on page 53. Brush the top crust with the egg wash. Place the pie on a baking sheet to collect any juices that bubble over. Bake for 30 minutes, then reduce the heat to 350°F (175°C) and bake for 30 minutes more.

Transfer the pie to a cooling rack and allow to cool for 20 minutes. Serve warm. The pie will keep for up to 4 days, covered, in the fridge.

FORAGING IN MODERN TIMES

When I'm at home on my parents' farm, dinner is easy. I can take a tour of the fields, listening to my dad's stories of weather woes and bug struggles, and fill a basket with whatever strikes my fancy—still-muddy potatoes, lima beans in the shell, tomatoes in every shade, succulent baby butternut squash. Then when I get into the kitchen, all I have to do is heat up my dad's big cast-iron frying pan, melt some butter, chop some garlic and herbs, and start sautéing. Sometimes a venison sausage, donated to the family in exchange for hunting privileges on our land, will make it onto the dinner plate, or a cut of pork from the heirloom pigs my sister raises will be the star of the meal. But more often than not, dinner is a glorious pile of vegetables.

The fields are so bountiful that sometimes I forget to notice the purslane underfoot, or the wild mustard greens that blur the boundaries of my dad's work and Mother Nature's beneficence. There's a whole world of wild food that complements the food we cultivate, and fortunately there are also some very charming and knowledgeable guides to help us navigate that world.

Sarah Kelsen is an ecological engineer and wild food expert located in Ithaca, New York. She leads her clients on nature walks, sharing her knowledge of edible wild plants along the way. On a springtime walk with Sarah, she led me to a small pond surrounded by cattail reeds. As a kid, my siblings and I loved to shred apart the flowering spikes of cattails and watch the cottony fluff float away in the breeze, but little did I know of their versatility. Sarah explained that cattails are not only a crucial wetland plant; they also have long been appreciated by Native Americans as a

source of food, medicine, weaving material, insulation, and even absorbent diaper stuffing. My first thought upon looking at the dried reeds and learning that cattails were edible was how unpleasant the fluff would be in my mouth. But of course, the fluff is not the edible part. Sarah crouched down and showed me where to look for new shoots among the dried reeds. We reached into the cold water to the base of the shoot and broke it away from its rhizome. Each shoot has several layers, like a leek, and the innermost layers are the most tender. Before we tasted the shoots, Sarah took a moment to thank the cattail for being such a generous provider. We peeled away a couple layers and munched on the delicate shoot. The flavor, similar to that of a cucumber, is mild, and it can be eaten raw or gently cooked.

Milkweed, the sole food source for monarch butterflies, is also edible, and several bushes were growing not far from the cattails. In the spring, the tender buds at the top of the plant have a flavor and texture somewhere between steamed broccoli and okra. Sarah noted that while it's fine to enjoy the delicate buds, we must remember not to take too many from a single plant and to share them with the monarch caterpillars.

Away from the pond and into the woods, Sarah pointed out the garlic mustard plants lining the edge of a trail. While we were conscientious about how much we took from the milkweeds and cattails, she encouraged me to uproot the whole plant and take as much as I wanted. Garlic mustard is an invasive species that takes over the forest floor and crowds out native plant species, so we're doing good work to diminish its presence. The leaves add a pungent kick to salads and pesto, while the roots can stand in for wasabi and horseradish.

Later in the summer I came to Ithaca once again and joined a group of would-be foragers for another one of Sarah's walks. This time we spotted green walnuts, which can be made into *nocino*, a bittersweet digestif, or allowed to ripen and painstakingly cracked to reveal nuts with an earthy, autumnal flavor that's impossible to describe. We found some black raspberry bushes, and I did my best not to eat them all on the remainder of the walk.

After the walk was complete, Sarah told me to follow her on a drive to a lakeside park where there was an especially bushy juneberry tree. We spent twenty minutes filling baskets with the berries, but the tree was so prolific that it looked as if we had scarcely unburdened its branches of fruit. Juneberries, also known as serviceberries or saskatoons, are native to the northern United States and Canada and often used for landscaping in parks and parking lots. The fruit resembles a blueberry, but it's more closely related to apples and pears. The taste is familiar, bringing to mind a cultivated blueberry crossed with a pear, with a subtle almond undertone. After I learned about juneberries from Sarah, I started noticing the trees elsewhere, even back home in Brooklyn. I love making pie with them (see page 70).

Foraging isn't just for rural areas. Wild foods can be found smack-dab in the middle of New York City, and "Wildman" Steve Brill can help you track them down. He does weekly tours in Brooklyn's Prospect Park, Queens' Forest Park, and Manhattan's Central Park in an effort to help city dwellers get back in touch with nature. His daughter, Violet, grew up assisting her dad with his tours, and now as a young teenager she leads her own tours. I attended one of Steve's tours of Central Park in the height of summer with about twenty other curious city folk. Steve showed us the wealth of wild foods underfoot (tangy wood sorrel and common plantain), overhead (Kentucky coffee pods and fuzzy red sumac clusters), and everywhere in between. He shared burdock jerky and Kentucky coffee truffles, and an extensive repertoire of dad jokes.

After my walks with Sarah and Steve, I knew that my next visit to my family's farm would not just be spent in the fields, but also walking through the woods and keeping an eye out for some of the wild foods I'd learned about. I wanted to find the wild pawpaws (a native fruit, also known as a custard apple, that has a musky flavor somewhere between an overripe banana and a mango) my dad was so fond of, and some persimmons if I could. Luckily my niece Ezra is an expert in the forest around her home and was able to lead us to a thicket of pawpaws teeming with ripe fruit, and several neighbors told us they were overwhelmed with persimmons on their properties. Both made their way into pies, of course.

When we talk about connecting with our food and learning where it comes from, the focus is often on local farms, which is wonderful. But our connection to sustenance can be even more profound and direct than a trip to the local farmers' market. Learning about wild foods alters your relationship to food and nature in subtle but powerful ways. It turns a walk in the park into a joyful exploration; it transforms your sustenance into a connection with the earth. It not only enhances your culinary creativity, it awakens you to nature's all-encompassing presence, power, and generosity.

QUICHE

Makes one 9-inch (23-cm) quiche

5 eggs

⅔ cup (165 ml) heavy cream

½ cup (120 ml) whole milk

¾ teaspoon salt

Mixture of vegetables, cheese, and/
or meats of your choice (see sugges-
tions on page 219), enough to fill the
pie pan

1 bottom crust, crimped (½ recipe any
crust type; see pages 50 and 52)

QUICHE CAN BE PRETTY POLARIZING—PERHAPS YOU THINK YOU don't like it because you've had ones that are rubbery, bland, and full of overcooked vegetables. Quiche is one of the simplest and most delicious ways to turn foraged greens (like the milkweed buds shown opposite) or seasonal vegetables into a quick meal. This recipe has plenty of heavy cream, which lends a luscious texture and satisfying richness. I encourage you to improvise with whatever vegetables, cheeses, or cooked meats you have on hand—this one recipe will get you so much mileage! My favorite combinations of ingredients are listed on page 219.

Preheat the oven to 400°F (205°C).

In a medium bowl, beat the eggs until the whites and yolks are well integrated. Add the cream and whisk until the color is uniform, followed by the milk and salt.

Place your choice of fillings into the bottom crust, then pour the egg mixture on top, making sure to scrape the entire contents from the sides of the bowl into the pie.

Bake for 15 minutes, then carefully remove from the oven. Tent a large sheet of foil loosely over the quiche, tucking the corners gently under the pie pan. Take care not to let the foil touch the surface of the quiche, and don't put any pressure on the crust, which will be very soft. Place the pan back in the oven and reduce the heat to 350°F (175°C). Bake for 50 minutes more, or until the surface of the quiche has puffed up and become golden near the edges.

Transfer the pie to a cooling rack and allow to cool for at least 20 to 30 minutes before serving. Serve warm or at room temperature. The pie will keep for up to 4 days, covered, in the fridge.

MUSHROOM AND CHIVE

¾ cup (25 to 50 g) sautéed mushrooms (enoki, thinly sliced cremini, or shiitake)

3 tablespoons chopped chives

½ cup (55 g) shredded Gouda

SUN-DRIED TOMATO AND SAUSAGE

⅓ cup (80 g) ricotta cheese

¼ cup (30 g) sliced oil-packed sun-dried tomatoes

½ cup (70 g) crumbled cooked Italian sausage

2 tablespoons slivered basil leaves

LORRAINE

¾ cup (80 g) grated Gruyère cheese

¾ cup (170 g) cooked bacon, chopped in small pieces

⅓ cup (80 g) caramelized onions

WINTER SQUASH

⅔ cup (75 g) grated winter squash (kabocha, butternut, or any sweet and nutty orange-fleshed squash will do)

2 tablespoons minced marjoram

⅓ cup (40 g) crumbled chèvre

FORAGED GREENS

½ cup (60 g) farmers' cheese

¾ cup (40 g) foraged greens (thinly sliced ramps or cattail shoots, milkweed buds, mustard greens, and/or fiddlehead ferns)

POTATO AND LEEK

½ cup (85 g) grated Yukon gold potato, sautéed in 2 tablespoons unsalted butter

½ cup (45 g) very thinly sliced leeks

½ cup (50 g) grated Parmigiano-Reggiano or Pecorino cheese

CHICKEN POT PIES

Makes 10 individual 10-ounce (280 g) pot pies

12 ounces (340 g) Yukon Gold potatoes

12 ounces (340 g) root vegetables (carrots, golden beets, or parsnips)

12 ounces (340 g) onions

4 cloves garlic

One 4- to 5-pound (1.8 to 2.3 kg) chicken

2 tablespoons salt, plus more to taste

2 teaspoons freshly ground black pepper

6 tablespoons (80 g) unsalted butter, cut into twelve pieces

8 ounces (225 g) seasonal vegetables (such as spring peas, zucchini, or winter squash)

4 ounces (115 g) leafy greens (destemmed thinly sliced kale or collards, or tender young spinach)

¼ cup (30 g) cornstarch

¼ cup (60 ml) heavy cream

¼ cup (15 g) minced seasonal herbs

1½ recipes Butter Pastry Dough (page 38)

Egg Wash (page 56)

AT PETEE'S, WE HAVE A PRETTY LABOR-INTENSIVE WAY OF MAKING chicken pot pies, but it's worth it. We start by roasting whole chickens (local and free-range, of course), then we use the bones and skin to make a rich stock and gravy, while the meat goes into the filling. The recipe changes throughout the year depending on the herbs and vegetables that are available. The result is a wholesome, comforting meal that is at home in any season. I've outlined our process here, but if you'd like to make shortcuts, that's okay, too! Simply use 3 pounds (1.4 kg) cooked chicken meat and 3 cups (720 ml) broth, and roast the potato, root vegetables, onions, and garlic on their own while you prepare the rest of the ingredients.

Preheat the oven to 400°F (205°C).

Peel the potatoes, root vegetables, and onions, and cut them into ½-inch (12-mm) pieces. Reserve the skins and scraps of the onions and root vegetables to use for the broth later. Peel and mince the garlic, reserving the skins as well.

Place the chicken in a large roasting pan and sprinkle it with 1 tablespoon salt and 1 teaspoon pepper. Roast for 30 minutes, then add the diced potato, root vegetables, onions, and garlic to the pan. (If you are using winter squash, peel and dice it to the same size and add it now as well.) Dot the vegetables with the butter, then sprinkle with 1 tablespoon salt and 1 teaspoon pepper. Return the pan to the oven and roast for 30 minutes more. Remove the roasting pan from the oven and let cool. Turn off oven while the stock cooks for 1 hour.

Once the chicken and roasted vegetables are cool enough to touch, transfer the vegetables and any juices from the pan into a large bowl. Remove the chicken skin and place it in a large stock pot. Remove the meat from the bird and set it aside on a cutting board. Break the chicken carcass up so that the bones fit compactly in the pot. Add the reserved vegetable scraps to the stock pot, then add enough water to cover the bones. Heat the pot over high and bring just to a boil, then cover with a lid and reduce the heat to low and simmer for at least 1 hour.

While the stock simmers, tear or cut the chicken meat into bite-size pieces and add it to the roasted vegetables in the large bowl. Dice the seasonal vegetables and leafy greens into ½-inch (12-mm) pieces, and mix them into the meat and roasted vegetables.

If baking the pies immediately, preheat the oven to 400°F (205°C).

When the stock is done simmering, put the cornstarch in a separate large bowl. Whisk in the cream to make a slurry. Gradually whisk 1 cup (240 ml) stock into the slurry until smooth. Whisk in another 2 cups (480 ml) stock until smooth. (The remaining stock can be reserved for another purpose.) Pour the liquid over the chicken and vegetable mixture, add the herbs, and stir everything together. Taste the filling and season with more salt as desired.

Divide the filling among ten 10-ounce (280 g) ramekins. Roll out the butter pastry to ¼ inch (6 mm) thick (using the method on page 50) and cut out shapes that will cover the ramekins.

Top the ramekins with the dough. Cut a couple of vents in each crust. The unbaked chicken pot pies can be wrapped in foil and stored in the freezer for up to 2 months.

To bake immediately, place the ramekins on a baking sheet, then brush the pastry with the egg wash. Bake for 30 minutes, or until the filling is bubbling and the crust turns deep golden. To bake from frozen, bake for 45 minutes at 400°F (205°C). Serve hot. The pies will keep for up to 4 days, covered, in the fridge.

À LA MODE

TOPPINGS & OTHER DELICIOUS HOMEMADE PIE INGREDIENTS

In his 1936 obituary in the *New York Times*, a professor named Charles Watson Townsend was credited with "inadvertently [originating] pie à la mode." He frequented the Cambridge Hotel in Cambridge, New York, in the 1890s and would order apple pie with ice cream for dessert. Another diner, Mrs. Berry Hall, called the dessert "pie à la mode." Directly translated from French, "à la mode" means "in the style," or "in fashion," but adding "à la mode" was simply a way of imparting an air of elegance onto a dish. Townsend went on to order the dessert by that name at the famous Delmonico's in New York City. As legend has it, he shamed the staff of such a distinguished gastronomic institution for being ignorant of this decadent dessert. In their embarrassment, they vowed to include pie à la mode on the menu henceforth—where it remains today, alongside baked Alaska and New York cheesecake.

So, we could keep New York in the center of the story and leave it at that. However, a *St. Paul Pioneer Press* reporter read the obituary and was compelled to repudiate it. He published an alternate origin story three days later. He claimed that a decade or so before Townsend ordered pie and ice cream in upstate New York, it was already a hit at Hotel La Perl in Duluth, Minnesota.

The chef-owner at the Hotel La Perl, Swiss-born John Gieriet, spent some time in France before immigrating to the United States. After several years as director of food service at the White House under Presidents Pierce and Buchanan, he moved to Duluth, Minnesota, and bought the Commercial Hotel, which he renamed Hotel La Perl. He converted the hotel's bar into a restaurant befitting of a chef of his stature and became known for throwing elegant dinners that he concluded with blueberry pie and ice cream, which he called "pie à la mode."

Personally, I want to know a little bit more about Berry Hall and her whereabouts before she mysteriously whispered "pie à la mode" after Professor Townsend placed his seemingly novel order. Had she passed through Duluth, Minnesota, perhaps?

Regardless, pie à la mode was an inevitable marriage of two beloved desserts. The textures, temperatures, and flavors of freshly baked pie and ice cream contrast and complement each other so perfectly. For this reason, it behooves any baker to have an excellent vanilla ice cream recipe to rely on. You don't have to stop there, though. At Petee's we offer both Vanilla Bean Ice Cream (page 229) and Maple Whipped Cream (page 228) as options, and I always admire the boldness of the rare customer who orders both on one slice. Beyond ice cream and whipped cream, a humble slice of pie can be dressed up decadently with any of the toppings we normally associate with a sundae, from chocolate fudge to cherries to crunchy roasted nuts. In this section, you will find recipes that can be used on their own to top pies or combined to create a luscious pie sundae. You will also find recipes for other important toppings and components that are necessary to make different pies throughout this book, such as meringue, homemade condensed milk, and more.

BUTTERSCOTCH SAUCE

Makes 1 cup (240 ml)

Butterscotch is essentially a caramel made with brown sugar instead of white sugar, so it has a distinct molasses flavor. It's great on any of the nut pies (pages 190–197), the Autumn Pear Pie (page 92), or the Salty Chocolate Chess Pie (page 176). Add a touch of booze if you want the sauce to have a little extra kick—I prefer aged applejack.

¼ cup (½ stick/55 g) unsalted butter

½ cup (110 g) packed dark brown sugar

1 teaspoon sea salt

½ cup (120 ml) heavy cream

1 teaspoon vanilla

1 tablespoon applejack, whiskey, or rum (optional)

In a heavy medium-size saucepan, preferably light in color so that you can see the color of the sauce as it cooks, combine the butter, brown sugar, salt, and heavy cream. Cook over medium heat, stirring constantly, until the butter is melted and the sugar is dissolved.

Bring the mixture to a boil. Let it boil for 4 or 5 minutes, scraping the sides of the pan with a rubber spatula occasionally to prevent burning.

Remove from the heat and stir in the vanilla and liquor of your choice, if using. Don't worry if this mixture is not thick—it will thicken as it cools. Serve warm.

The sauce will keep for up to 2 months in an airtight container in the fridge. Warm the sauce on the stove over low heat to your desired temperature before serving.

Pie sundaes, top to bottom: Apple Pie with Vanilla Bean Ice Cream, Cajeta, and pepitas; Lemon Chess Pie with torched meringue and Wild Blueberry Sauce; Salty Chocolate Chess Pie with Maple Whipped Cream, Macerated Cherries, and Butterscotch Sauce; and Brown Butter Honey Pecan Pie with Maple Whipped Cream and Hot Chocolate Fudge

CAJETA

Makes 2 cups (480 ml)

Cajeta is a Mexican caramel made from goat milk. It's similar to dulce de leche, but thanks to the wider range of amino acids present in goat milk, it's more interesting and complex. I admit it's not a traditional pie topping or sundae component, but it's excellent drizzled over pie and ice cream nonetheless—I love it on apple, sweet potato, and pecan pies. It can be also be used as an ingredient in pies, such as the Cajeta Marlborough Pie (page 172) and Cajeta Macadamia Pie (page 188).

½ teaspoon salt

2 cups (400 g) sugar

1 teaspoon baking soda

8 cups (2 L) goat milk

2 cinnamon sticks

1 vanilla bean, seeds scraped and saved

In a large, heavy pot, whisk together the salt, sugar, and baking soda. Whisk in the goat milk, cinnamon sticks, and vanilla bean pod and scrapings. Cook over medium heat, stirring regularly with a spatula, until the sugar is completely dissolved and the mixture starts to foam and bubble, about 15 minutes.

When the mixture starts to bubble, keep a close eye on it: It can boil over quickly, so be ready to turn off the heat and let it settle before returning it to a lower heat. If the heat is too high it will boil over, but if it's too low it will take forever for the mixture to reduce. Keep the heat high enough to maintain a strong simmer for 45 minutes to 1 hour, stirring frequently and scraping the sides and bottom of the pan with the spatula to prevent burning. The mixture will develop a golden caramel-brown color and thicken to a caramel-sauce consistency. It should coat the back of a spoon, and the final volume should be about 2 cups (480 ml).

The cajeta will keep for up to 3 months in an airtight container in the fridge, or up to 1 year in an airtight container in the freezer.

CHOCOLATE FUDGE

Makes 1½ cups (360 ml)

Chocolate fudge is a classic sundae component, and it also goes nicely with a wide range of pies. Try it on any nut or custard pie, or even cherry pie or cheesecake.

¾ cup (180 ml) heavy cream

2 tablespoons unsalted butter

½ cup (110 g) packed light brown sugar

⅛ teaspoon salt

1 ounce (30 g) dark chocolate, chopped

½ cup (50 g) sifted cocoa powder

½ teaspoon vanilla

In a small saucepan, combine the cream, butter, brown sugar, and salt. Cook over medium heat, stirring constantly, until the butter has completely melted, then allow to simmer for about 1 minute.

Remove from the heat and stir in the chopped chocolate until melted. Whisk in the cocoa until fully incorporated.

Return the pan to low heat. Whisk until the sauce is completely smooth and glossy, under a minute. Remove from the heat and whisk in the vanilla. Serve warm.

The fudge sauce will keep for up to 2 months in an airtight container in the fridge. Warm the sauce on the stove over low heat to your desired temperature before serving.

CUSTARD SAUCE

Makes 1¼ cups (300 ml)

Custard sauce, or crème anglaise if you're fancy, is popular in England, where you can find it on anything from rhubarb crumble to mince pies. Custard recipes often require tempering, a method in which a portion of the hot mixture of dairy and sugar is added incrementally to the egg yolks to prevent them from curdling. As shown in this recipe, it's possible to make this custard sauce without tempering the egg yolks, as long as you have a candy thermometer to keep you in line and you can quickly chill the custard in an ice bath. I love custard sauce on Rhubarb Pie with Brown Butter Hazelnut-Almond Streusel (pages 66 and 59) and Black Currant Pie (page 82).

Ice water

⅓ cup (65 g) sugar

6 egg yolks

¾ cup (180 ml) heavy cream

1 cup (240 ml) whole milk

½ vanilla bean

Pinch of salt

Place a metal bowl in the sink or in a larger bowl filled with ice water.

In a medium saucepan, whisk together the sugar and egg yolks until smooth. Gradually whisk in the cream, then whisk in the milk.

Scrape the vanilla bean and add the contents and the pod to the saucepan, along with the salt.

Cook over low heat, stirring constantly with a rubber spatula, until the mixture reaches 170°F (76°C). (At 180°F/82°C, the yolks will start to scramble.) Remove from the heat and immediately pour the custard into the metal bowl. Discard the vanilla bean pod. Stir the mixture for about 1 minute to aid cooling.

Spoon the custard sauce over the pie while it is still warm, or chill the custard sauce completely in the fridge, if you prefer it cold. (It will become thicker in the fridge but still be pourable.)

The sauce will keep for up to 1 week, covered, in the fridge.

HOLIDAY CUSTARD SAUCE VARIATION

For a festive, wintry variation—excellent on everything from Persimmon Pudding Pie (page 162) to Mince Pie (page 105)—add ⅛ teaspoon nutmeg while cooking the custard and stir in ½ teaspoon orange zest while it cools.

MACERATED CHERRIES

Makes 1 cup (250 g)

These cherries can be used for more than just Nesselrode Pies (page 136); try them in cocktails and sundaes, or even make them into a confection by dipping them in melted dark chocolate. The extra syrup can be used in homemade sodas or in a champagne cocktail.

1 pound (455 g) pitted sour cherries

1⅓ cups (265 g) granulated sugar

3 tablespoons dark rum

2 tablespoons confectioners' sugar

2 tablespoons cornstarch

In a large saucepan, combine the cherries, granulated sugar, and rum. Cook over medium-low heat for 45 minutes, stirring every 5 minutes, until the cherries are tender, and the syrup is thin and have the color of red wine. Don't let the mixture boil, but if it does, turn down the heat.

Preheat the oven to 200°F (90°C).

Strain the cherries, saving both the syrup (for cocktails or to serve over ice cream) and the cherries. Transfer the cherries to a mixing bowl.

In a small bowl, whisk together the confectioners' sugar and cornstarch. Sift the sugar mixture over the cherries, and toss to coat.

Place the cherries on a baking sheet and bake for 2 hours. The cherries will darken slightly in the oven and have a drier, stickier texture as some of the moisture evaporates. The cherries can be kept in an airtight container in the fridge for up to 2 weeks, and the syrup can keep in the fridge for up to a month.

MAPLE WHIPPED CREAM

Makes 1¼ cups (300 ml)

Using maple syrup in place of regular sugar just makes whipped cream better! Whipped cream is usually made with confectioners' sugar, lending it a somewhat stiff texture. Since maple syrup is fluid, it makes a softer whipped cream, but with a superior flavor. I love adding maple whipped cream to Pumpkin Pie (page 170), Sweet Potato Pie (page 164), and any chess pie (pages 178–186).

1 cup (240 ml) heavy cream

¼ cup (60 ml) maple syrup

Contents of ½ of a vanilla bean

Pinch of salt

In the bowl of a stand mixer with the whisk attachment or in a large bowl with a hand-held mixer, whip all the ingredients together, moving gradually from low to high speed. Whip until desired texture is achieved. Enjoy it on the same day it's made—it tends to separate after sitting in the fridge for more than a day.

SOUR CHERRY OR WILD BLUEBERRY SAUCE

Makes 2 cups (400 g)

When you order a slice of cheesecake at Petee's, you get the option to add a topping of sour cherry or wild blueberry sauce, both of which provide a fruity contrast to the rich dairy flavors in the cheesecake. These sauces also taste amazing on pie sundaes.

SOUR CHERRY SAUCE

½ cup (100 g) sugar

3 tablespoons cornstarch

Pinch of salt

12 ounces (340 g) pitted sour cherries, fresh or frozen

2 tablespoons lemon juice

WILD BLUEBERRY SAUCE

¼ cup (50 g) sugar

1 tablespoon cornstarch

Pinch of salt

12 ounces (340 g) wild blueberries, fresh or frozen

3 tablespoons lemon juice

Combine the sugar, cornstarch, and salt in the bottom of a medium saucepan. Add the fruit and toss to coat in the dry ingredients, then add the lemon juice and 3 tablespoons water. Heat over medium-low heat, stirring constantly with a rubber spatula, until the juice has started to come out and the fruit is warm (about 5 minutes for fresh fruit and 10 to 15 minutes for frozen). Increase heat to medium and continue to stir until the mixture comes to a simmer and has bubbled for about 5 minutes. The sauce is done when it's slightly thick and the juices are no longer cloudy from the cornstarch. Remove from heat and allow to come to room temperature before transferring to an airtight container and chilling completely, about 1 hour, in the fridge. The sauce will thicken a little more as it cools, but it will remain fluid enough to spoon over cheesecake or sundaes. Keep for up to 1 week in the fridge.

VANILLA BEAN ICE CREAM

Makes 1 quart (960 ml)

This is a custard-style ice cream that churns up rich and smooth. Simmering the vanilla bean pod in the custard imparts it with a distinct vanilla flavor.

Ice water

½ cup (100 g) sugar

4 egg yolks

1¼ cups (300 ml) heavy cream

⅔ cup (165 ml) whole milk

½ vanilla bean

⅛ teaspoon salt

½ teaspoon vanilla

Place a metal bowl in the sink or in a larger bowl filled with ice water.

In a medium saucepan, whisk together the sugar and egg yolks until smooth. Gradually whisk in the cream, then whisk in the milk.

Scrape the vanilla bean and add the contents and the pod to the saucepan, along with the salt.

Cook over low, stirring constantly with a rubber spatula, until the mixture reaches 170°F (76°C). (At 180°F/82°C, the yolks will start to scramble.) Remove from the heat and immediately pour the custard into the metal bowl. Discard the vanilla bean pod. Stir the mixture for about 1 minute to aid cooling, then stir in the vanilla extract.

Cover the bowl with a lid or plastic wrap and transfer to the fridge to cool completely before churning. Churn according to the instructions for your ice cream maker. Store in an airtight container in the freezer. The flavor and texture are best when eaten within 1 month.

OTHER DELICIOUS HOMEMADE PIE INGREDIENTS

In this section are recipes for two great ways to top pies, chilled ones in particular—meringue and whipped cream—plus ingredients that will come in handy for making pies throughout the book. I'm a stickler for using high-quality local dairy, but the option isn't always available, like in evaporated milk and sweetened condensed milk. Making these yourself can take a little time, but it allows you to have the utmost control of their quality—and save some money to boot. The mainstream organic brands can be quite expensive.

EVAPORATED MILK

Makes 1½ cups (360 ml)

This one is very simple! Evaporated milk is an important ingredient in the custard pies (see page 158–160), because it gives the fillings a rich dairy flavor without overwhelming fattiness.

3¼ cups (780 ml) whole milk

In a medium pot, cook the milk over medium heat until it just starts to simmer, then immediately reduce the heat to low and simmer until it has reduced to 1½ cups (360 ml), around 30 minutes or more depending on your stove, the saucepan, and the ambient temperature. The most important thing is to keep the heat low enough that the milk doesn't boil, which causes it to separate. Let the evaporated milk cool before using; it will keep up to 2 weeks in an airtight container in the fridge.

SWEETENED CONDENSED MILK

Makes 1¾ cups (420 ml)

Brilliant pastry chef Stella Parks discovered that adding a portion of heavy cream to the milk and sugar before condensing prevents burning. Use this in Key Lime Meringue Pie (page 130) and any other recipes that call for sweetened condensed milk.

3 cups (720 ml) whole milk

½ cup (120 ml) heavy cream

¾ cup (150 g) sugar

In a large saucepan, combine the milk, cream, and sugar and cook over medium heat, stirring often, until the mixture simmers and the sugar has dissolved. Cook for 30 minutes more, scraping the bottom of the pot with a rubber spatula to prevent burning. It will start to foam up when it is almost done. The texture will be slightly thinner than canned sweetened condensed milk, but it will thicken to a similar texture as it cools. Let the sweetened condensed milk cool before using; it will keep up to 1 month in an airtight container in the fridge.

VANILLA SEA SALT MERINGUE

Makes 5 cups (1.2 L)

This Italian meringue is a little bit more labor-intensive than an ordinary meringue, but it is silky smooth and versatile. Not only can it be used to top lemon or key lime pies, it is beautiful on chocolate and coconut cream pies as well. Since the egg whites are cooked by the hot sugar syrup, this meringue can be enjoyed by the spoonful on top of a slice in place of whipped cream, without any further cooking. It's especially delicious on autumnal custard pies such as Persimmon Pudding (page 162), Pumpkin (page 170), and Sweet Potato (164). Halve the recipe to use it as a topping.

½ cup (120 ml) egg whites (equivalent of 3 large egg whites), at room temperature

½ teaspoon cream of tartar

1 cup (200 g) sugar

½ teaspoon vanilla

¼ teaspoon sea salt

Make sure the egg whites are completely free of any yolk and that your bowl and mixer attachments are completely clean and nongreasy. Otherwise, the egg whites will not whip properly.

In the bowl of a stand mixer with the whisk attachment or in a large bowl with a hand-held mixer, beat the egg whites and cream of tartar on high until they are white and foamy and hold soft peaks.

Meanwhile, in a saucepan, stir ¼ cup (60 ml) water and the sugar over high heat until the sugar has dissolved and the syrup reaches a strong boil. The temperature on a candy thermometer should read 240°F (116°C). Remove from the heat.

With the mixer running, pour the hot sugar syrup in a thin stream into the foamy egg whites. Continue beating until the meringue holds the pattern of the whisk or beater as it spins. The texture should be voluminous but still silky.

Add the vanilla and salt and beat just until combined.

Use the meringue immediately to assemble a meringue pie according to the instructions in the recipe, or use as a pie sundae topping.

LEMON POPPYSEED MERINGUE VARIATION

Fold 2 tablespoons poppyseeds into the meringue before topping the pie. They add an elusive earthiness and charming aesthetic.

VANILLA WHIPPED CREAM

Makes 2½ cups (600 ml)

This whipped cream is made with just enough confectioners' sugar to have a nice, solid structure that allows it to hold up on top of a pie, but not enough to become too sweet. A touch of salt and nice dose of vanilla extract round out the flavor. It's great on any of the cream pies, and it's also tasty on the lemon curd (see page 128) or the key lime custard (see page 130), if you want to forgo meringue. For a topping or serving alongside pies such as pumpkin, see page 228 for my lighter, softer version of whipped cream.

1½ cups (360 ml) heavy cream

½ teaspoon vanilla

Pinch of salt

⅓ cup (40 g) confectioners' sugar

In a large bowl or the bowl of a stand mixer, combine the cream, vanilla, and salt. Sift in the confectioners' sugar. Using a hand-held mixer or the whisk attachment, beat on high until the cream is voluminous and still holds its shape but is smooth.

RESOURCES

INGREDIENTS

In my culinary experience, there's nothing more joyful than getting food straight from a farmer and turning it into a pie. Depending on where you live, you can do this by taking a trip to a local farm, visiting a farmers' market, or buying from a farm online. Here are a few ideas:

I'm not an expert in other cities' farmers' markets, but in New York City, Union Square Greenmarket usually has every seasonal fruit and vegetable I could ever want, and then some! There are a number of stands selling a great selection of heirloom and modern apple varietals, as well as purveyors of local grains, honey, maple syrup, and responsibly raised meats.

In Los Angeles, the Santa Monica Farmers Market has a glorious array of fruits, vegetables, nuts, seafood, and cheeses: smgov.net/portals/farmersmarket. Plus, you might get the chance to meet Lety Garcia at the Garcia Organic Farm stand!: @garciaorganicfarm on Instagram.

FRUIT

Pick your own apples at Samascott in Kinderhook, New York: Samascott.com/pyo; and at Locust Grove Farm in Milton, New York: LocustGroveFruitFarm.com.

Frozen wild blueberries by mail: BlueHillBerry.com/store.

Frozen black currants (and tons of other black currant products!) by mail: CurrantC.com.

Frozen sour cherries can be purchased year round at Singer Farm in Appleton, New York: SingerFarmNaturals.com/cherries.

NUTS

We buy organic pecans for Petee's directly from Green Valley Pecans. They grow both conventional and organic pecans, which can be purchased on their website: PecanStore.com.

Missouri Northern Pecan Growers is a farmer cooperative that sells organic and conventional pecans, as well as pecan oil: mopecans.com.

DAIRY

If you live in an area where there are dairy farms, of course I encourage you to buy local butter. If not, you can buy excellent butter from independent farmers online, if you wish. To make the shockingly good butter crust at Petee's, we use Kriemhild butter: KriemildDairy.com.

You can buy delicious milk, cream, yogurt, and butter from Ronnybrook in New York and beyond: Ronnybrook.com.

GOODS AND SUPPLIES

Freshly milled organic New York flours: FarmerGroundFlour.com.

We use Jonathan's wild cherrywood pie servers to dish out pie at Petee's: WoodSpoon.com.

My late friend and ceramics teacher Wynne Noble left behind a beautiful legacy of handmade ceramic dishes. You can buy ceramic pie dishes and beautiful dessert plates made in her studio by her lovely crew: NoblePlateware.com/shop.

INFORMATION AND EDUCATION

Food history websites: researchingfoodhistory.blogspot.com, foodtimeline.org, RachelLaudan.com

For a window into the gastronomic proclivities of bygone years, check out the New York Public Library menu database: menus.nypl.org.

New York foraging experts:
Steve Brill in New York City: WildmanSteveBrill.com.
Sarah Kelsen in Ithaca: wildflx.com.

Petra "Petee" Paredez, enjoying the sunshine outside of our Clinton Hill, Brooklyn, café

THANK YOU

To the Petee's staff: for bearing with our growing pains and helping us be better every day. I cannot believe our luck in finding all of you beautiful, intelligent people to work with every day.

To my parents: for being unbelievably hard-working and showing us how to make an honest living selling pie—not to mention our dear Artofex, the produce, and material support.

To my children: for helping me keep it all in perspective, making life beautiful, and being excellent pie models.

To Robert: for being the best possible partner in business and life; for all your thoughtfulness and intelligence, and your patience, which gives me room to grow.

To GDA: for your enthusiastic help in getting our business off the ground.

To Cindy Uh: for searching me out and having faith in my ability to write something worthwhile.

To Christine Zulkosky: for helping me write the proposal for this book.

To all the farmers featured in this book: for sharing with me your knowledge, your invaluable time, and the fruits of your labor.

To Maya and Lizzie: for generously sharing your home with us. It's the perfect backdrop for pie!

And finally, to Laura Dozier and the Abrams team: for valuing my perspective and making this beautiful book happen.

INDEX

235

Editor: Laura Dozier
Designer: Jennifer Wagner
Production Manager: Denise LaCongo

Library of Congress Control Number: 2020931031

ISBN: 978-1-4197-4758-8
eISBN: 978-1-64700-014-1

Printed and bound in the United States
10 9 8 7 6 5 4 3 2

Abrams books are available at special discounts when purchased in quantity
for premiums and promotions as well as fundraising or educational use.
Special editions can also be created to specification. For details, contact
specialsales@abramsbooks.com or the address below.

Abrams® is a registered trademark of Harry N. Abrams, Inc.

ABRAMS The Art of Books
195 Broadway, New York, NY 10007
abramsbooks.com

*The material contained in this book is presented only for informational and artistic purposes.
If you use plants or flowers for any of the recipes included in this book we suggest you use only
items from farmers' markets or grocery stores. If you choose to eat plants or flowers you may
have found in the wild, you are doing so at your own risk. The author has made every effort to
provide well researched, sufficient, and up-to-date information; however, we also urge caution
in the use of this information. The publisher and author accept no responsibility or liability for
any errors, omissions, or misrepresentations expressed or implied, contained herein, or for any
accidents, harmful reactions, or any other specific reactions, injuries, loss, legal consequences,
or incidental or consequential damages suffered or incurred by any reader of this book. Readers
should seek health and safety advice from physicians and safety professionals.*